INCLUSIVE ECONOMICS

Inclusive Economics

Gandhian Method and Contemporary Policy

Narendar Pani

Los Angeles | London | New Delhi
Singapore | Washington DC | Melbourne

Copyright © Narendar Pani, 2001

All rights reserved. No part of this book may be reproduced or utilised in any form or by any means, electronic or mechanical, including photocopying, recording or by any information storage or retrieval system, without the permission in writing from the publisher.

First published in 2001 by

SAGE Publications India Pvt Ltd
B1/I-1 Mohan Cooperative Industrial Area
Mathura Road, New Delhi 110 044, India
www.sagepub.in

SAGE Publications Inc
2455 Teller Road
Thousand Oaks, California 91320, USA

SAGE Publications Ltd
1 Oliver's Yard, 55 City Road
London EC1Y 1SP, United Kingdom

SAGE Publications Asia-Pacific Pte Ltd
18 Cross Street #10-10/11/12
China Square Central
Singapore 048423

Published by Vivek Mehra for SAGE Publications India Pvt Ltd and typeset in 10.5/12.5 pt Baskerville Win95BT by Line Arts, Pondicherry.

Library of Congress Cataloging-in-Publication Data

Pani, Narendar, 1954–
Inclusive economics: Gandhian method and contemporary policy/Narendar Pani.
 p. cm.
Includes bibliographical references and index.
 1. Gandhi, Mahatma, 1869–1948—Contributions in economics. 2. Economists—India.
 3. Economics I. Title.
HB126.153G367 330'.0954-dc21   2002   2001048424

ISBN: 978-07-619-9580-7 (HB)

SAGE Team: Abantika Chatterji, Arpita Das, O.P. Bhasin and Santosh Rawat

In Memory of Dayanand Pani

The analytical mind has so much more to it than the science it creates.

Thank you for choosing a SAGE product!
If you have any comment, observation or feedback,
I would like to personally hear from you.

Please write to me at **contactceo@sagepub.in**

Vivek Mehra, Managing Director and CEO, SAGE India.

Bulk Sales

SAGE India offers special discounts
for purchase of books in bulk.
We also make available special imprints
and excerpts from our books on demand.

For orders and enquiries, write to us at

Marketing Department
SAGE Publications India Pvt Ltd
B1/I-1, Mohan Cooperative Industrial Area
Mathura Road, Post Bag 7
New Delhi 110044, India

E-mail us at **marketing@sagepub.in**

Subscribe to our mailing list
Write to **marketing@sagepub.in**

This book is also available as an e-book.

Contents

Preface	9
1. The Case for Inclusiveness	13
Why Gandhi?	
2. Primacy of Action	36
Improving Subjectivity/The Concept of Knowledge/Truth and Faith/Evaluating an Action	
3. Economic Action	61
Choice of Objectives/Trusteeship/Swadeshi/Choice of Actions/ Gandhi and his Method	
4. Methodological Outposts	91
Choice of the Problem/Models and Explanation/ The Demarcation Question/Dealing with Subjectivity/ The Challenge of Rhetoric/The Role of Interpretation/Method of Intervention/Approaches to Conflict	
5. Departure from Convention	129
The National Economy/The Institutional Framework/ The Preoccupation with Growth/Consequences versus Key Factors/Absorbing Specialisation/The Ideological Divide/ The Individual and the Firm/The Gandhian Corporation/ Combating Expediency	
6. In Practice	161
The Indian Budget of July 1991/A Methodological Critique/ A Gandhian Alternative	
7. In Conclusion	189
Select Bibliography	195
Index	201
About the Author	207

Preface

The conventional route to Gandhi's ideas is through the man. Typically a fascination with Mahatma Gandhi and his ideals leads to an urge to explore his ideas. This is not the route this book has taken. The roots of this book lie in the environment of economics academia in India in the 1970s. It was a time when Indian economists were paying a great deal of attention to village studies. Some economists argued with much conviction, and not a little vehemence, that village studies were the only meaningful way to understand the rural Indian economy. Implicit in this approach was a near contempt for studies based on secondary data. As a student of economics struggling to put together an acceptable Ph.D. thesis it seemed obvious that neither methodological technique was free of risk. No matter what the quality of the insights one received from a village study, there was always the risk that one would be studying an exception rather than the rule. And no matter how comprehensive an exercise based on secondary data, there was always the risk that the sharp variations that exist on the ground would be summarised into a meaningless average. We could end up like the marksman who misses his target first by two feet on the right and then by two feet on the left, but believes it does not matter as the average is on target. An awareness of these risks led to a search for a more inclusive method that would be comprehensive even as it retained the benefits of a much narrower focus.

The immediate response to the need for an inclusive method was to simply put together information from as many sources as possible. This rudimentary inclusiveness did have its uses. In a study of land reforms in the south Indian state of Karnataka, the use of historical information alongside contemporary secondary data served to completely alter the perception of the problem. When the focus was on secondary data alone, it was assumed that the landlord-tenant relationship was an approximation to the relationship between the lord of the manor and the serf. But when the historical picture was taken into account it became clear that tenancy had no such connotation. The tenant was just as likely to be a dominant farmer as an impoverished one. The landowner too had often leased out his land only because he did not have the resources to cultivate it himself.

Gaining this insight and convincing peers about it were, however, two entirely different things. The degree of rigour tended to vary depending on the source of information. It was not always possible to carry out on historical information the kind of rigorous statistical testing that was possible with contemporary secondary data. And how could others be certain that the choice of information with varying degrees of rigour had not been guided by expediency? Clearly, if one had to have a hope of convincing others, one had to identify an inclusive method that economists would find acceptable. It was in this search that one went into Gandhi's ideas in some detail and emerged convinced that if we could distil his method from his voluminous writing, it could provide the framework for an inclusive economics.

This route to Gandhi's ideas distances this work from that of those who began with a fascination with the Mahatma. It does not share the traditional Gandhian's fondness for asceticism. It is also acutely aware of the difference between Gandhi's methods and his judgements. It recognises that it is possible to accept his method even without supporting all his judgements. And it is more concerned with the contemporary economy than it is with the economy of Gandhi's time.

In taking this alternative route I have benefited greatly from intellectual support received from a variety of sources. Professor

N.C.B. Nath and Dr M.G. Narasimhan went through early drafts and left one convinced that much work remained to be done. Dr Ramachandra Guha went through a later draft but had the same effect. Dr Anandlingam and Dr Deepa Ollapally kept the book growing through continuous disagreement. Mr Georgy Thomas used his editing skills to make the book more accessible. Seminars at the Institute for Social and Economic Change and the National Institute of Advanced Studies, helped clarify several aspects of the problem.

When pursuing a problem of this kind over so many years a price is paid by those who are closest to you. Jamuna, Sharat and Sarayu paid that price cheerfully.

1

The Case for Inclusiveness

As the Asian crisis unfolded after Thailand was forced to let the baht float on 2 July 1997, it raised an issue on which there was rare unanimity among economists. Major economists of otherwise different persuasions agreed that they had not anticipated the crisis.[1] Those who celebrated the Asian 'miracle' earlier were undoubtedly the ones who were most perplexed. But even critics of the earlier performance were not fully equipped to answer the questions that the crisis raised. One of the foremost of these critics, Paul Krugman, admitted the Asian crisis took them by surprise (Krugman, 1998a).[2] While they expected a conventional currency crisis, what they got was one that did not follow the patterns laid out by standard currency crisis models. There was no fiscal imbalance on the eve of the crisis, the inflation rates were low, there was no substantial unemployment and the economies seemed to have already completed a boom-bust cycle. Krugman, in fact, went on to suggest that these unexpected developments were not necessarily an exception: 'As is all too often the case, we find ourselves playing theoretical catch-up—trying after the fact, to develop a framework for thinking about events that have already happened' (ibid.).

In itself, this collective failure is no more than a reminder that even economists are fallible. All sciences come up against phenomena that they have not previously encountered. In fact, it is often through understanding previously unknown phenomena that a science develops. And it did not take very long for economists to come up with explanations for the various dimensions of the Asian crisis. The debilitating impact of panic in the markets, the moral hazard created by guarantees, the asset bubbles that resulted from crony capitalism, as well as the effects of competitive devaluation, were quickly analysed with precision and in detail. The technological ground opened up by the internet even allowed for the discussion on the Asian crisis to become, arguably, the first near real-time debate in economics.[3] It is thus quite tempting to dismiss the collective failure of economists to anticipate the Asian crisis as no more than a short-lived embarrassment.

And yet, hidden in the very swiftness of the response is a less comforting thought: If economists could come up with comprehensive explanations so quickly, what stopped them from arriving at these theories before the crisis took place? This question gets even more intriguing when we consider the fact that many of the concepts used to explain what happened in Asia were known before the crisis. Competitive devaluation, crony capitalism, moral hazard, panic in the markets and several other concepts used to analyse the Asian crisis were not unknown before July 1997. What is it then that prevented economists from using their knowledge to anticipate the crisis?

The obvious answer is that economists either underestimated the factors that caused the crisis or that these factors behaved in ways that were not anticipated. Soon after the crisis broke out, Jeffrey Sachs spoke of 'two kinds of optical illusion' that lay behind it (Sachs, 1997). First, large capital inflows led to currency appreciation. But such short-term currency appreciation did not offer an accurate picture of future relative prices, thereby misleading investors. Second, newly liberalised banks played a major role in channelling foreign funds into the domestic economy. But these banks often operated under highly distorted incentives. As the owners of the banks had little of their own capital at risk in the lending, they were not as prudent as they should have been. To the two kinds of 'optical illusion' that Sachs listed, others can be added. For instance, there was the policy makers' 'optical illusion' that devaluation helped exports, when it only led to competitive devaluation.

The interesting aspect of these 'optical illusions' was that they were not created by the emergence of previously unknown economic phenomena. Recognising these illusions for what they were did not require any fundamentally new concepts in economics. These 'optical illusions' were the result of the same factors, which economists had analysed in great detail, behaving differently in a new context. The 'optical illusions' thus emphasised the fact that economists could fail not only when there were factors at play they knew nothing about, but also when known factors behaved differently in a different context. After this experience, the situational dimension of economic relationships cannot be dismissed as a relatively minor detail. If economists are not to be surprised by events, they need to recognise that their theories can function very differently as situations change.

This is so simple, and obvious, a contention that few economists dealing with the real world would question it. They do, after all, have to understand an economy before deciding what is best for it. But absorbing this situational dimension fully into economics is not always easy. The situational dimension can come into conflict with some established elements of economists' method. And one element that does, in practice, work against economists' ability to anticipate a new situation is an excessive commitment to their favourite models. Most economists, understandably, seek to abstract a few relationships in order to understand them better. This abstraction is essential to bring in the required degree of rigour. But abstraction involves focusing on some elements of a situation and ignoring others. The choice of these elements necessarily makes a difference to the understanding of the situation. And the appropriate choice could vary from situation to situation. The choice of a model with one set of elements may be crucial to the understanding of a particular situation, but very much less relevant in another situation. In a situation where inflation is caused by excess liquidity, a model focusing on controlling money supply may be the most appropriate input. But in a situation where inflation is caused by supply bottlenecks this would not be the case. Too great a commitment to a model could then adversely affect the ability to understand diverse situations. And even if economists were able to overcome their commitment to a particular model, how would they choose the set of minor models that are needed to make up the larger picture of the economy?

Those fascinated with models would try to answer this question by building a larger model that links the minor ones. The larger model would have to be comprehensive enough to take into account all the factors that influence a particular issue, as well as how they operate in different situations. This approach would cover a wide range of models from Marx to Walras, Hicks and Leontief. These larger models together represent, to use Morishima's broad definition of the term, a General Equilibrium Approach. Defined in this broad way this approach covers the thinking of some of the greatest minds of the nineteenth and twentieth centuries. And yet, despite the many significant advances provided by each of these models, this approach has not led to an unchallenged, truly comprehensive, picture of the economy. 'All of these views are entirely pertinent', as Morishima points out, 'but each by itself is essentially a distortion, seeking out no more than a single facet of reality' (Morishima, 1992, p. 69). There is thus little in the history of economic thought to suggest that a new model can be developed that will understand all factors in all situations. Indeed, if that were to happen it may well be the end of economics, as economists would have no more answers to find.

In the absence of a distinct objective method of putting together models to form a comprehensive picture of the economy as a whole, economists tend to follow their own preferences. The models that are put together to form the larger picture tend to be determined by the world view of the economist concerned. The picture of the economy as a whole drawn up by Monetarists consists of one set of models, while the picture developed by Keynesians consists of another set. And other practising economists could come up with yet another set. Economists would argue that this choice of models is not entirely random.

As the quality of models improves, in terms of both rigour and empirical testing, it gets more difficult for individual economists to completely ignore one or the other set. Even those who are not a part of the Monetarist tradition, for instance, will accept that a sharp increase in money supply, without a corresponding increase in output, will exert an upward pressure on prices. Over time the number of models that gain such wider acceptance can be expected to grow. Krugman has endorsed this process by acknowledging that in the initial years what is lost through the narrowness of a formal model may be more than what is gained. But, he argues, this picture gets better as more rigorous models are developed to understand different aspects of the economy (Krugman, 1994).

Appealing as Krugman's description of the process of gaining knowledge in economics may be, it leaves too many questions unanswered. Can we be certain that new models will necessarily improve the overall picture and not distort it? Even a model that is accurate in itself could distort the larger picture by drawing attention to inconsequential factors. Sometimes, given economists' penchant for sophistication, a complex model could easily attract greater attention than it deserves in terms of the overall picture of the economy. How are we to then decide how relevant a particular model is to understanding a given situation? The judgements of individual economists on the relevance of a model to a situation can, and do, differ. And even when there is unanimity, it could turn out to be a case of collective failure, as in the inability of economists to anticipate the Asian crisis.

The answers to these questions require a closer look at the methodology of economics than most economists discussing policy are willing to take. Despite the revival of interest in economic methodology since 1980, policy makers continue to have little time for issues of method. They evidently believe the adage that those who do, do and those who don't, discuss methodology.[4] In terms of their attitude to economic methodology, economists dealing with policy issues have not moved very far from the view expressed by Irving Fisher in his famous presidential address to the American Statistical Association in 1932:

> It has long seemed to me that students of the social sciences, especially sociology and economics, have spent too much time in discussing what they call methodology. I have usually felt that the man who essays to tell the rest of us how to solve knotty problems would be more convincing if he first proved out his alleged method by solving a few himself. Apparently those would-be authorities who are forever telling others how to get results do not get any important results themselves (cited in Hoover [1995]).

Implicit in this rejection of methodology is the view that the value of economists is determined by their ability to solve practical problems. The value of an economic theory is then, correspondingly, dependent on its practical results. Ironically enough, in taking this view, Fisher and his modern followers are making a statement of method. Indeed, their view is almost identical to that of the American philosophical school of Pragmatism. It is, in fact, a restatement of the basic principle of Pragmatism, first enunciated by Charles Sanders Peirce in 1878. Put simply, this principle states that the value of an idea lies in its practical results (Passmore, 1968, p. 109). Thus economists who claim to shun method do not really do so. All that they do is to accept, without critical examination, the traditional position of Pragmatism. Economists who are sceptical about the value of general theories and also shun discussing methodology, are thus only moving from the General Equilibrium Approach to Pragmatism.

This shift from the General Equilibrium Approach to Pragmatism is mirrored in the realm of economic policy making. The General Equilibrium Approach translates in the realm of policy making to what can be termed an ideological approach. Though the term ideology implies much more than a single general theory, economic policy makers who are identified with an ideology try to remain consistent with the general economic theory at the core of that ideology. This tendency may be most evident among Marxists, but Keynesians, Monetarists and those owing allegiance to a variety of other schools of thought also tend to reduce reality, wherever possible, to the core theory they believe in. The core general theory provides the theoretical framework into which individual policies can be fitted. The weakness that Morishima referred to, of each of these theories dealing only with a single facet of reality, is thus transmitted to the ideological frameworks of policy makers. It is then hardly surprising that, sooner or later, policy makers come up against situations that are not easily explained by their core ideological theory. And, in practice, policy makers have found it difficult to ignore the inadequacies of each of these theories for long.

The obvious example of these inadequacies is the collapse of communism. But the problems were not confined to this ideological framework alone. In fact, signs of dissatisfaction within each ideological framework were visible before the collapse of communism. Well before Mr Gorbachev initiated the chain of events that led to the break up of the Soviet Union, there were very few examples around the world of economies strictly following ideological economic models based on a completely free market or on complete state control. There was a role for private ownership within the communist bloc, though the nature of this role varied from country to country.[5] In the free market economies too there was a fairly significant role for the state, though this role differed quite sharply between countries committed to a welfare state and others more keen to allow a free hand to the market.[6] Specific economic models that emerged from one ideological tradition could then be quite relevant to economies that were supposedly committed to the opposite ideological tradition. The growing role of free markets in communist countries was accompanied by demands for protection within the advanced capitalist world. Indeed, the World Trade Organisation (WTO) interpreted the Most Favoured Nation status in a way that allowed countries within a regional bloc greater access to each other's markets than countries outside the bloc.[7]

Even when the political situation did not allow the abandoning of ideology, there were signs of an erosion of faith in the economics of that ideology. Old parties with old ideologies were quite willing to absorb elements from opposing ideological frameworks.[8] Deng Xiao Ping led the effort of the ruling party in China to incorporate the market into its view of communism. The need to incorporate market reforms into old ideologies may have been relatively less obvious in India. But when the then Indian Finance Minister, Dr Manmohan Singh, launched his economic reforms in a speech presenting the country's budget in 1991, a significant part of that exercise went into insisting that the new policies were only a continuation of the old.[9] Where there was no old ideological baggage, policy makers were careful not to put on new ideological straitjackets. In some cases this took the form of simply doing what was expedient. For instance, neither a free market ideology nor the ideology of state ownership could effectively justify some states in East Asia supporting business houses of their choice.[10] In other cases, it took the form of policy makers keeping their options open rather than opting for a single ideological model. This was most evident in the realm of international trade. The United States, for one, kept open the option of unilateralism through the 1990s with its 301 trade legislation even as it strengthened regionalism through Nafta and played a major role in determining the course of multilateralism through the WTO.[11]

The rejection of ideological frameworks forced policy makers to find an alternative mechanism of moving from their specific models to the larger reality. Without the need to even pretend to be following a particular ideology, policy makers secured the flexibility to put together packages of policies based on individual formal theories. In picking the theories to be used, there was no longer any reason to consider whether the chosen theory originated from one ideological position or the other.[12] Policy makers could also follow a particular policy and then reverse it when the situation changed.[13]

But in putting together such packages the policy maker still had to justify how he came to pick one set of options over another. For a while there was an attempt to underplay the extent of the shift from the old ideology. In the last two decades of the twentieth century, political parties across the world claimed to continue following a left-wing ideology even as they aggressively moved towards the market. This was clearly the case both with the Communist Party in China and, to a lesser extent, the Labour Party in Britain. But over time the difference between the ideological framework and the practice of the government became too glaring to ignore. The policy maker had to then justify this difference. And more often than not the only justification offered was that the changed policies had to be judged in terms of the effects they had. As Deng Xiao Ping argued famously, the colour of the cat did not matter as long as it caught mice. In other words, the only justification policy makers offered was that the policy was pragmatic.

The parallel shift to Pragmatism in both mainstream economics and policy making occurred without widespread debate. In a science famous for aggressive debate this shift took the form of a quiet movement from one conventional wisdom to another. The smoothness of this transition must not, however, lead to an underestimation of its significance. This transition represented a fundamental break in the way economists moved from their specific models to the larger picture of the economy. As a result of this transition, the larger picture is less frequently drawn on the basis of a particular theory. Instead, the focus is on the pragmatic method of choosing a set of models. The focus has quietly shifted from justifying an action because it was consistent with a particular theory to justifying it because it was picked pragmatically. The prime concern of economists and policy makers has shifted from general theories to method.

This shift in focus from the General Equilibrium Approach, and ideological theories, to method has several significant consequences. First, it opens the policy making process to pluralism. In ideologically determined policy making, individual policies are expected to be consistent with the core ideological theory. Any action that is inconsistent with the core ideological theory can, at best, be an exception and not the rule. But when the emphasis shifts to method, the policy maker no longer needs to be committed to a single theory. He can choose any model that he believes would be most appropriate to achieve results. The choice of models would vary depending upon the criteria used. Criteria that are only concerned with the condition of the poor will throw up one set of policies while criteria based on the belief that nobody should be worse-off could result in another set.[14] And even when the same criteria are used, the prescribed policy package could vary. It would be influenced, for instance, by the knowledge available. The choice of policy cannot be independent of the quantity and quality of empirical information available about a specific situation. The shortfall in knowledge could also be the result of the inadequacies of theories existing at a point of time.[15] In such situations of imperfect information, economists can, and do, find it difficult to agree. And since there is no way of knowing for certain which set of policy prescriptions is the best before they are implemented, economists have to come to terms with a multiplicity of analyses at each point of time. This pluralism substantially increases the number of options the economic policy maker can consider. He has the option of choosing one model in a particular situation and a completely different one in another situation. Pragmatism is thus better equipped to address the situational dimension of economics than the old General Equilibrium Approach or ideological theory.

A second consequence of the shift from the General Equilibrium Approach and ideological theory to method is in the way economists and their theories are perceived. As long as policies are being justified on the basis of ideological theories, economic policy makers can be divided along ideological lines. But once the focus shifts to the method of choosing a set of policies, new divisions arise between followers of one methodology and another. These boundaries cut across old ideological boundaries. Certain elements of method could be common to policy makers following radically different ideologies. Marxists and free marketers can, and often do, have the same faith in falsification. This could alter the interpretation of terms like 'mainstream'. Traditionally, Marxists may have considered the supporters of free market economics to comprise the mainstream. But when the dividing lines are drawn in terms of method, the term will have to refer to all those who share the method that is accepted in economic establishments across the world. Incidentally, as this is a study in method, the term mainstream will be used in the latter, broader, sense.

A third, and arguably the most important, consequence of the shift from theory to method is that methodological issues can no longer be brushed aside. What should be the basis for economists to move from their specific models to the general economy? This question becomes particularly important in a situation where the focus of the models is narrow. If economists can speak with certainty only about the narrow area of their specialisation, how do they relate to other areas of the economy? And if they are to put together the specialised work of others, what are the criteria they should use? Without answers to these questions, the combination of theoretical and empirical rigour makes formal economics very good at explaining events that have occurred. But its narrow focus makes it rather less effective in predicting situations that have not been previously known.

When it is evaluated as a method of moving from a specific economic model to a larger picture of the economy it is evident that much of the criticism that Pragmatism faces in the realm of philosophy is relevant to its more mundane economic counterpart. In particular, Pragmatism in economic policy would be open to the charge of expediency that several of the early American Pragmatists faced.[16] The principle of deciding a policy on the basis of the effects it would have creates room for expediency. While the effects will be clear after the policy is implemented, i.e., ex post, the policies have to be determined before they are implemented, i.e., ex ante. It is then possible to follow inefficient, expedient policies as they will only be detected much later when the effects are visible.

The choice of the expedient option, over the one that provides the best results for the economy, could be prompted by a variety of motives. In some cases, there could be a direct material benefit for the policy maker. The obvious example is crony capitalism. In other cases, the benefit need not immediately take a material form. An economist who is identified with a particular theory may like to ensure that that theory becomes the basis for policy, even if he is not absolutely certain it will actually work. And in yet other cases, the expedient option could be chosen simply because it is the easiest to convert into policy. This would be the case when policy makers choose an inappropriate option simply because they have not bothered to collect sufficient information.

That these are not just some abstract possibilities is evident from two well documented trends in the 1990s. First, within individual countries expediency allowed state support to be provided to specific business houses, resulting in cronyism in some East Asian economies.[17] Apart from the ethical problems involved in such expedient relations between the state and private capital, the inherent economic problem of moral hazard pushed the economies towards a crisis. The protection provided by the state made these investors oblivious to the costs and risks of their investment decisions. And when these costs rose to a point where the state could no longer absorb them, the economy was plunged into crisis.[18]

Second, at the global level, the expediency of policy makers in individual governments introduced imperfections into the functioning of the world market. China's devaluation of the yuan in the process of unifying its currency in 1994 suited its interests quite admirably. It gave it an edge over most of its competitors, particularly those in East Asia. Indeed, there is a school of thought that believes that this devaluation was a factor in the crisis in East Asia.[19] What may have been expedient for China was clearly not so for several other Asian economies.

The damage that expediency causes can completely erode the benefits of Pragmatism. The flexibility that allows Pragmatism to take into account a larger number of factors in a way that is sensitive to the situational dimension can become a source of misuse of policy-making powers. The freedom to move beyond the confines of an ideological theory means very little if it only results in policy being determined by the personal interests of the policy maker. Thus, even as the inadequacies of the General Equilibrium Approach, and ideological theories, gain wider recognition, Pragmatism is not the alternative.

This brief outline of the inadequacies of the General Equilibrium Approach and Pragmatism serves a purpose beyond rejecting these two methods. It also points to the conditions that a viable alternative must satisfy. If economists are not to be caught by surprise, as they were in the Asian crisis, they would need a method that overcomes the inadequacies of these two approaches. When stated in this form it is clear that our focus is on predictability in economics. This is not to presume that such a focus alone is relevant. Economists can, and do, have an eclectic approach to the purpose of their activity. Sometimes the purpose could be such that predicting crises is not the prime concern. An economist working on making a specific model more rigorous may not be interested in the predictability of that model in a specific situation. But economists who develop policy in pursuit of specific objectives need to be able to predict the results of their policies, particularly if there are undesirable consequences. The inadequacies we had identified in both the General Equilibrium Approach and Pragmatism have thus been primarily from the point of view of policy makers. Consequently, the requirements that we now go on to identify for an effective alternative method are also from the perspective of economic policy makers alone.

The inadequacies of the General Equilibrium Approach and Pragmatism centre around their inability to address two issues. First, both methods fail to ensure comprehensiveness in the analysis of factors in a particular situation. Different General Equilibrium Approaches concentrate on different factors. Pragmatism has the flexibility to switch from one set of factors to another. But there is nothing in the method itself that specifies that all factors, major and minor, must be taken into account. The method can then be reduced to choosing one set of factors or another as the only factors that are important enough to be considered. And this choice can easily be distorted by expediency.

Second, both methods fail to provide an adequate response to the situational dimension of economics. For a method to be valid for all situations it needs to understand all factors that could be important in all conceivable situations. Some General

Equilibrium Approaches, like Marxism, do claim such completeness. But the collapse of communism has raised doubts about the validity of such claims. Pragmatism can claim to be more sensitive to the situational dimension. Since it has the freedom to operate with different sets of models in different situations, it can come up with a situation-specific analysis. But there is no way of being sure that the analysis of a situation has not been distorted by expediency of one kind or another.

An effective alternative method must then address the twin issues of comprehensiveness and being sensitive to the situational dimension. Comprehensiveness would involve taking into account all factors that could play a role in a particular situation. The method would then demand an understanding of how these factors interact with each other. It would recognise the fact that factors that were previously insignificant can become significant in a new situation. Towards the end of the twentieth century the importance of the environment in economic analysis is not doubted; but just a few decades earlier it was treated as a minor externality. And even when a factor continues to be minor in itself, it could interact with other factors in a way that significantly transforms the overall picture. The material used to package a particular product is often only a minor factor in determining the economic fortunes of that industry. But in a situation where manufacturers are forced by the market to use a material that is not easily available to some of them, this minor factor could have a significant impact on the industry as a whole. The alternative method must then include all factors, both major and minor, and then understand their interaction with each other.

The alternative method must also be sensitive to the situational dimension. As the method needs to take into account minor factors as well, there can be an infinite number of possible situations in different economies at different points of time. It would then be difficult, if not impossible, to predetermine each type of situation. What is needed instead is a set of criteria by which different models can be put together in order to understand a particular situation. Such a set of criteria should, ideally, allow the method to not only address a specific situation but also predict future scenarios that could arise from the situation. The alternative method must then be inclusive both in terms of the factors it considers as well as the situations it can address.

As the focus of this inclusive method is on putting together models in order to understand a specific situation, its emphasis must be on the criteria to choose models rather than any particular model. It cannot be too attached to any particular set of theories. It must be willing to change models either because the situation changes or because better models become available. This inclusive method thus need not present a completely different set of economic theories. It only needs to present a different method of using economic models.

In meeting the conditions of inclusiveness it is important that the method does not compromise on the strengths of earlier approaches. In particular, the search for inclusiveness must not compromise on the rigour that has characterised the General Equilibrium Approach. If there exists a rigorous understanding of an economic relationship, the inclusive method cannot accept an understanding of that relationship if it does not stand up to the same degree of rigorous analysis. But the search for rigorous analysis cannot become an excuse to ignore factors that could be crucial in understanding a situation. The lack of adequate information or scope for rigorous analysis cannot override the demand for inclusiveness. The inclusive method would then tend to move into areas mainstream economics is not keen to enter. As it enters uncharted waters it must be particularly aware of the role of expediency. It must identify the scope for expediency and then develop mechanisms to reduce it, if not eliminate it altogether!

An obvious place to begin the search for an inclusive method would be the vast body of literature on economic methodology that has emerged after 1980.[20] This literature covers a wide range of issues that are needed to develop an alternative methodology. It goes beyond the objective aspects of economic thinking to an evaluation of the subjective dimensions. It explores the role of rhetoric and interpretation. To this body of literature can be added developments in other fields of economics that could be modified to address issues in economic methodology. The theory of choice from welfare economics, for instance, could be of some relevance to the choice of the appropriate model, or set of models, for a particular situation. This very significant body of literature must be tapped in the search for an inclusive alternative to the General Equilibrium Approach and Pragmatism.

But in utilising contributions on specific issues to develop an inclusive method, we return to the old problem that eroded the value of both the General Equilibrium Approach and Pragmatism. How does one put together the individual elements to arrive at an inclusive methodology for policy makers? The existing debate on economic methodology does not provide an easy answer to this question, largely because an inclusive method meeting the requirements of policy makers is not a great priority for the participants. In some cases, the focus of the participants is on specific questions of method rather than comprehensiveness. The distance between the participants in this debate and those seeking an inclusive methodology becomes even greater when we recognise that comprehensiveness for a policy maker includes issues not only in the formulation of a policy, but also in its implementation. There is, for instance, little evidence of those interested in the debate on falsification finding time to consider the intricacies of collective action. Others are certainly more inclusive, seeking out new aspects of economic methodology. McCloskey's work on rhetoric, for instance, brings in dimensions of economic analysis that traditional economists would ignore. But while these contributions are more inclusive, they do not always share the concerns of the policy maker. McCloskey, when building his case for the study of rhetoric, argues that 'science is writing with intent, the intent to persuade other scientists, such as economic scientists' (McCloskey, 1994, p. 320). But this focus on how economists convince other economists, while being important, is not always the prime concern of policy makers. They are more likely to be concerned about how economists convince policy makers and how policy makers convince their target audience.

There are thus no ready-made solutions available within mainstream economics to the search for an inclusive methodology. While many of the elements of such a methodology have certainly been explored in considerable detail, there is still a need for a framework to put together a complete inclusive method for economic policy makers. And there is no reason to confine this search to mainstream economics. As we are looking for a method of putting together individual models rather than a completely developed alternative economics, we could easily find inclusive frameworks from other fields, or thinkers, that can serve a positive purpose in mainstream economics. The raison d'être of this work is to argue that the Gandhian method provides precisely such a framework.

WHY GANDHI?

The choice of Gandhi as the thinker whose ideas would be of use to post-communist economics may surprise many traditional economists. There has been a strongly held view that whatever Gandhi's contributions may have been to politics or ethics, he had very little to offer economics. The attitude of mainstream economists to Gandhian thought often borders on ridicule, as is evident from this assertion by a historian of Indian economic thought:

> Railways have spread the bubonic plague and increased the frequency of famines in India, machinery is a 'grand yet awful invention'; a doctor or a lawyer should be paid the same wage as a labourer, the law of supply and demand is 'a devilish law', tractors and chemical fertilizers will spell ruin for India. It is for voicing opinions such as these that Gandhi as an economist is remembered. Even a sympathetic reader may find it difficult to take such statements at their face value. This could explain why, although Gandhi has come to be accepted world-wide as one of the outstanding political and moral thinkers of our time, his economic thought attracts little attention (Dasgupta, 1993, pp. 131–32).

Others have been less harsh on Gandhi's economic views, but they too tend to stress the impracticality of it all. This could be suggested by the choice of words as in the reference to 'Gandhi's idealization of the village community' (Gadgil and Guha, 1993, p. 181). At a less direct level, the same impression is conveyed through the identification of Gandhian thought with specific actions he advocated in the specific situation he faced decades earlier. For instance, Bhabatosh Datta outlined the 'basic principles' of the Gandhian economic programme to be:

> ...first, avoidance of mechanisation and encouragement of cottage industries...; second, improvement of rural small scale agriculture; third, making the village community as much self-sufficient and self-reliant as practicable; fourth, decentralisation of the administrative and economic structure; fifth, reducing income inequalities, by raising the income level among the poor and by changing the attitude and motivation of the rich; and sixth, ensuring that capitalists and big businessmen serve as 'trustees' for the whole community (Datta, 1978, p. 152).

These 'basic principles' could, at best, be pious objectives. They have little prospect of success in the real world. Mechanisation is an essential part of modernisation, agriculture can be more productive when carried out on a large scale, isolating each village can prevent it getting the benefits of globalisation, decentralisation of the economic and administrative structure is only now being attempted in a rather rudimentary form in India and few big businessmen offer to become 'trustees' of their businesses. And if all that Gandhi had to offer was a set of principles he would have liked to see in an economy, he has no place in the world of economists trying to understand how an economy functions.

The trouble with all these views, irrespective of the degree of sympathy they profess for Gandhian thought, is that they seek to draw from Gandhi's actions a theory that is valid for all times and all situations. The search for such a theory is flawed on several counts. Gandhi repeatedly emphasised the situational dimension in his analysis. Even if we assume that not all his actions were situational, it is difficult to decide which action was valid in all situations and which action was appropriate only for specific situations.[21] His ideas would thus be distorted if they are taken out of context and converted into absolute principles. Moreover, seeking to understand Gandhi's ideas in terms of the actions he advocated alone can be misleading. Gandhi was primarily a political activist advocating actions with the objective of achieving specific goals. Consequently, his actions could, at times, be determined by their political symbolism rather than their intrinsic economic value. In some cases the symbolism was obvious. The Salt Satyagraha, where Gandhi led a march to Dandi, was a symbol of the opposition to British rule and, more precisely, of the struggle of Indians to gain control over their own resources.[22] No one would interpret walking great distances to pick up a handful of salt as the most economic way of obtaining that commodity. But there were other areas where the symbolism was closely interlinked with an economic assessment. As we shall see later, Gandhi's advocacy of hand-spun cloth was both as a symbol of the Indian national movement as well as an alternative source of livelihood for the poor. In such cases, it is difficult to define where exactly the symbolism ends and economic rationality takes over.

Building theories on the basis of an evaluation of political actions is made more difficult in Gandhi's case because he often chose an action because it was desirable and not because it had the greatest chance of success. Gandhi's campaign for industrialists to become trustees of their own industries was based on his belief that it was desirable. Does the fact that he did not succeed in convincing a sufficient number of industrialists then mean that his reasons for considering this action to be desirable were wrong?[23] Sifting Gandhi's theories from his actions is thus a task made extremely difficult by the fact that Gandhi's actions not only had a strong situational and political dimension, but were also not based on the chances of their success alone. And even if we were to accurately identify all the theories underlying Gandhi's actions, their direct value in understanding a modern economy would be in some doubt. Gandhi's emphasis on the situational dimension would militate against transplanting those theories to a modern economy. His emphasis on the fallibility of knowledge would also mean that some of his theories could well be wrong. As we shall see later, Gandhi himself was wary of all-knowing theories of history.

Indeed, it is this scepticism about grand theories that makes Gandhi relevant to the challenges faced by economics at the beginning of the twenty-first century. Without a grand theory to fall back on in the face of previously unknown situations, Gandhi recognised the need to go beyond theories to the method of understanding society. The method he developed was inclusive enough to deal with both the known and the unknown, while reducing the scope for expediency. And since Gandhi believed in the primacy of action, it was a method best suited to the requirements of policy makers.

Once we shift the focus from Gandhi's theories to his method there is much wider acceptance of his ideas. Even within mainstream economics there is some, though not clearly defined, recognition of the value of the Gandhian method. Boulding, for instance, contended that 'the culture of the scientific community is profoundly Gandhian. It is based quite fundamentally on the principle that people should be persuaded by evidence and never by threat. The extraordinary success of science in expanding human knowledge is a direct consequence of this principle' (Boulding, 1992, p. 234). The rise of postmodernism, particularly outside economics, has also led to a wider recognition of the value of the Gandhian method. Pieterse argues that 'postmodern sensibilities have been voiced earlier or independently in non-Western points of view' and that Gandhi's 'views overlap with other emancipatory perspectives' (Pieterse, 1992, p. 30).

But our primary concern here is not with placing Gandhi in the context of late twentieth and early twenty-first century thought. It is not even to go into great detail into all aspects of Gandhian thought. The task we have set for ourselves is to see whether the Gandhian method would help economic policy makers make decisions on the basis of an inclusive approach. As a result many interesting issues will be of only peripheral interest in this book. The possibility that Gandhi may have anticipated many of the insights of post-modernism will be treated as incidental. Many critical elements of Gandhian thought, like *ahimsa,* too will find mention only to the extent that they influence the Gandhian method of understanding the economy. Even when Gandhi's ideas are being compared to other thinkers, like Popper, the focus will only be on their methods of understanding society. Other issues, such as the similarities or differences in their concepts of truth, are only analysed to the extent that they have a direct impact on their respective methods. When dealing with a thinker of Gandhi's versatility, it is important to stress at the outset that this work is concerned with nothing more than the utility of the Gandhian method to economic policy makers after the collapse of communism.

We begin this exercise by first outlining some of the premises of the Gandhian method in general, followed by its specific form in economics. We then proceed to record the response of the method to methodological issues that arise in the formulation and implementation of a policy. This is then followed by a review of the departures from the conventional in economics that results from the adoption of this method. These departures are illustrated by outlining a Gandhian alternative to the main policy statement that initiated economic reform in India in 1991. This is clearly a very wide canvas. In other words, this exercise itself follows the principle of inclusiveness. This allows us, at the end of the exercise, to list the benefits we have gained by following an inclusive method.

NOTES

1. As Radelet and Sachs (1998) have noted, the East Asian crisis is remarkable for a variety of reasons. It hit the most rapidly growing economies in the world, it prompted the largest financial bailouts in history and, of particular significance given the concerns of this book, it was the least anticipated crisis in years.

2. One analyst refers to Krugman as 'the only commentator who can be truly proud of what he wrote about Asia beforehand' (Frankel, 1998, p. 3).
3. Among the most active of the internet sites dealing with the crisis was the Asian crisis homepage, maintained by Nouriel Roubini.
4. Krugman, in fact, finds it necessary to acknowledge this adage before a very brief discussion on methodology in his paper on development economics (Krugman, 1994).
5. The economic reform of 1968 in Hungary, for instance, provided a role for the market even as the country remained within the Soviet bloc.
6. The extent of commitment to a free market within a capitalist economy could also change along with changes in the political leadership, as happened when Mrs Margaret Thatcher launched her drive for privatisation in the United Kingdom in the 1980s.
7. The most favoured nation clause in an international trade agreement requires signatories to offer to each other the same trading terms offered to a third country. But the WTO allowed countries within trading blocs to charge products from each other at a lower rate of tariff than that charged on products from countries outside the bloc. This was justified on the grounds that lower rates in even a part of the world market was a movement towards free trade. But it did help protect producers within the trade bloc from competing products from countries outside the bloc.
8. The phenomenon of old parties advocating new policies may be most visible in the case of communist parties adopting market reforms, as in China or Vietnam. But it is by no means confined to the remnants of the communist world. Many old parties in the rest of the world too have changed their attitude to the market. This is as true of Tony Blair's Labour Party in Britain as it is of the Congress Party in India after 1991.
9. This is discussed in greater detail in Chapter 6.
10. The chaebols of South Korea are among the examples cited most often of the marriage between the state and private enterprise.
11. These options were simultaneously kept open by emphasising the issues on which there was no conflict between the options. For instance, in May 1998, the United States put India on its Special 301 watch list for not providing adequate and effective protection for intellectual property rights (*The Economic Times*, Bangalore, 3 May 1998). But since on this issue the WTO was also likely to have held a position similar to that of the United States, there was no real conflict between unilateralism and multilateralism. And the scope for commonality between unilateralism, regionalism and multilateralism was enhanced by the way each of these systems worked. For instance, the dilution of the most favoured nation principle within the multilateral system, so that countries could offer additional concessions within a regional bloc, made regionalism consistent with multilateralism.
12. For instance, protectionism used to be associated with left-wing theorists fighting imperialism, but in the world after the fall of the Soviet Union, it was also advocated by the extreme right in the United States.

13. One of the main thrusts of India's economic reform was the removal of several restrictions on the foreign exchange market. But when the Asian crisis erupted, Indian policy makers responded by placing restrictions on the rupee.
14. This approximates to the choice between the Maximin and Pareto criteria in welfare economics.
15. Much as policy makers tend to treat the absence of information as primarily a problem of insufficient data, very often collecting accurate data does not solve the problem of adequate information. It is also important to first know what data should be collected and, once they are available, which set of relationships should be explored. And these questions are determined by the theories that are in place at that point of time.
16. Peirce, as well as other Pragmatists, recognised the need to address the question of Pragmatism opening the door to expediency. They worked towards a more precise definition of Pragmatism that would help remove the scope for expediency.
17. For an elaboration of the term 'crony capitalism', see Frankel (1998, p. 2).
18. For a more detailed model explaining how over-guaranteed and under-regulated economies can lead to excessive investment, see Krugman (1998a).
19. Among those who list this as a factor are Corsetti, Pesenti and Roubini (1998).
20. For a summary of some of the debates in economic methodology, see Backhouse (1994).
21. In theory, we could make use of A.K. Sen's distinction between basic judgements which are 'supposed to apply under all conceivable circumstances' (Sen, 1979, p. 59) and non-basic judgements which can change with circumstances. But in practice it would be very difficult to identify which specific actions of Gandhi were basic and which were not.
22. Though it took 17 years after the Salt Satyagraha for India to gain freedom, one biographer of Gandhi has argued that soon after the Satyagraha was over, 'India was now free. Legally, technically, nothing had changed. India was still a British colony. But there was a difference' (Fischer, 1954, p. 102).
23. Gandhi was himself often quite sceptical of his success in convincing individual industrialists (Gandhi, 1958–93, Vol. 90, pp. 521–22).

2

Primacy of Action

The Gandhian method is built around the cornerstone of the primacy of action. This is hardly surprising for a method developed by someone who intervened actively in political and social processes. But, for Gandhi, the primacy of action was more than a way of life, it was an article of faith. A devoutly religious man, he interpreted Hinduism in a way that stressed the importance of action. When listing what he considered to be the basic tenets of Hinduism, he stressed the belief that the soul takes on, from time to time, a body as a result of *karma* (in this context the sum of a person's actions in a previous existence) or the power of *maya* (illusion). It then 'goes on being born again and again into high or low species in accordance with the good or bad deeds performed by it' (Gandhi, 1958–93, Vol. 4, p. 408). The way to be liberated from this cycle of birth and death was 'to do good deeds, to have compassion for all living things, and to live in truth' (ibid., p. 408). Given this underlying faith, it is useful to begin our exploration of the Gandhian method with his concept of action.

In exploring the concept of action, as indeed in developing many other elements of his method, Gandhi relied on the Bhagvadgita.[1] The very nature of the Gita is such that it is open to diverse interpretations. It avoids simple definitions and concentrates instead on the specific elements of a concept.

Understanding concepts in the Gita is then the result of a continuous process where understanding the particular improves the understanding of the whole; which in turn improves the understanding of the particular, and so on. The understanding of a concept is thus prone to change both over time and across persons. Thus at any given point there could be several interpretations of a concept. What is under consideration here is only Gandhi's interpretation of the concepts in the Bhagvadgita, and not a general review of the many interpretations of these concepts.

Gandhi's translation and commentary on the Bhagvadgita suggests that he endorsed its definition of action: 'Knowledge, the object of knowledge, and the knower compose the threefold urge to action; the means, the action and the doer compose the threefold sum of action' (Bhagvadgita, Chapter XVIII, cited in Gandhi, 1996, p. 271). The most striking aspect of this concept of action is its inclusiveness. An analysis of an action using this concept would cover the entire range of issues that arise from the first idea that prompts an action to the consequences of the final act. The inclusiveness also ensures that the analysis is not confined to the objective elements, but also captures the subjective dimension reflected in the knower and the doer.

In evaluating an action, seen in these inclusive terms, Gandhi focused on its consequences. Several of Gandhi's choices reflected his emphasis on the consequences of an action. This is, perhaps, best seen in his view that a person of high moral standard 'will be considered guilty if he does not practice morality; but *nobody will find fault with him if his immoral behaviour has no consequences for society*' (Gandhi, 1958–93, Vol. 6, p. 332, emphasis added). Even actions that would normally be considered desirable, such as charity, were to be subject to an evaluation of their consequences. 'There is no reason to believe that charity per se is meritorious' (ibid., Vol. 28, p. 15) and there was a 'need for discrimination in practicing this virtue' (ibid., Vol. 28, p. 14). His focus on consequences led him to oppose the traditional Hindu custom of giving free meals to the able-bodied poor, believing that if food was available without effort, those who were habitually lazy would remain idle and become poorer (Dasgupta, 1993, p. 155). Gandhi's inclusive definition of action, in fact, ensured that the focus on consequences was applicable not only to physical actions but also to the thought processes that urged such actions. This meant the only knowledge that was worthwhile was that which was useful.

> We should remember that non-possession is a principle applicable to thoughts as well as things. A man who fills his brain with useless knowledge violates that inestimable principle (Gandhi, 1958–93, Vol. 44, p. 104).

This focus on consequences has sometimes led economic historians to argue that 'Gandhi ... shared with the mainstream economic tradition a consequentialist approach to choice' (Dasgupta, 1993, p. 137). And Gandhi's choice of actions were undoubtedly consistent with this definition of consequentialism: 'The rightness of actions—and (more generally) of the choice of all control variables—must be judged entirely by the goodness of the consequent state of affairs' (Sen, 1984, p. 278). But while Gandhi was sensitive to consequences, this in itself is not sufficient grounds for terming the Gandhian method consequentialist. Consequentialism requires not just an emphasis on consequences but also that no other criteria are needed to justify an action. As Sen points out: 'The importance of studying consequences need not be based on the acceptance of consequentialism, since a denial of consequentialism is a denial of the sufficiency of consequences for moral judgements, not of their necessity. There are, in fact, very few moral theories that are fully consequence-independent' (ibid., pp. 297–98).

To take a definitive view on whether Gandhi believed the goodness of consequences to be sufficient grounds to accept an action is difficult. As a practising politician, he had few opportunities to take an explicit position on such methodological issues. The specific choices he made, and his reasons for doing so, do point to the factors he took into consideration. But it would be very difficult to insist that no other criteria influenced a particular choice. This lack of clarity about what Gandhi really meant would be a severe handicap in a study of Gandhian thought. Our interest in the Gandhian method is, however, not so much for its own sake, but to see if it helps in developing an inclusive method for economics. The relevant question then is can we treat the goodness of consequences as a sufficient condition for deciding upon an action? If we answer this question in the affirmative, a number of concerns need to be addressed. And, interestingly enough, Gandhi did address these concerns.

The primary concern that arises from evaluating an action entirely in terms of its consequences is that it would ignore the rights of individuals. To use a particularly extreme example, if a specific type of society is considered good, would it justify annihilating individuals in the process of creating that society? Gandhi addresses this problem at several levels. To begin with, the inclusive nature of his method makes it impossible to identify either a pure action or a pure consequence. It is certainly possible to identify an action and its consequence in the abstract. But in reality all actions merge into consequences. To get back to our somewhat extreme example, the annihilation of an individual may be seen as an action designed to achieve the consequence of a better society. But for the person being annihilated, there is no difference between the action and the consequence; indeed it is the final consequence. In a society where there are numerous interrelationships, all actions will be indistinguishable from consequences. In Gandhi's words, 'There is no difference between means and ends' (Gandhi, 1958–93, Vol. 82, p. 446). Indeed, as is well known, Gandhi spent much of his life arguing that the ends could never justify the means. The means had to be good in themselves. In other words, if we consider an action and its consequence in isolation, the action must not just result in good consequences, but must also be good in itself. And actions that violate this condition are unlikely to be normally considered good. The consequentialism of the Gandhian method can then be extended to include the protection of rights.

But the protection of rights cannot be absolute. There could be rights which, when exercised, harm society. An action that grants each individual the right to destroy everyone else is unlikely to be considered good. The Gandhian method thus also requires criteria for deciding which rights are good. And the criterion set by the Gandhian method is that rights must be derived from duties.

Gandhi's case for linking rights to duties was a simple one. All rights are provided to individuals by society. For the society to continue to provide them, these rights had to be in the interests of not just the individual but also of society. As Gandhi put it: 'Fundamental rights can only be those rights the exercise of which is not only in the interest of the citizen but that of the whole world' (Gandhi, 1958–93, Vol. 88, p. 230). Society would then work towards protecting these rights. It is important to stress here that the role that society plays cannot be played by the state alone. Gandhi was, in fact, sceptical about how much the state could achieve on its own. The onus of protecting rights then falls primarily upon the individuals who together form society. The protection of rights is then the duty of individuals. And if individuals consistently fail to perform their duty towards the protection of a right, that right would automatically wither away. In Gandhi's words, '... all rights emanate from duties—if there is no duty, there is no right either' (ibid., Vol. 90, p. 91). 'The man who neglects his duty and cares only to safeguard his rights does not know that rights that do not spring from duties done cannot be safeguarded' (ibid., Vol. 88, p. 236).

The link between rights and duties in the Gandhian method is thus not a pious statement of intent. It is a practical means of ensuring that rights are safeguarded. As a practical weapon it is not sufficient to merely make a broad link between rights and duties. Each right has to be traced to a specific duty, or set of duties, that will protect it. The right to free speech, for instance, would only survive if individuals did their duty of not using speech in a way that is anti-social. Once free speech leads to anti-social behaviour, the very right will be questioned. Similarly, the right to a completely free market would be best protected if individuals did their duty of ensuring that markets did not destroy society. If markets are allowed to destroy society, the right to a free market will necessarily be challenged. Every time a duty is not performed, it erodes the ability of society to protect the corresponding right.

This negative statement has a positive corollary. If a society does not identify the specific duties required to protect a particular right, it would, in effect, be stating that that particular right was not worth having. As Gandhi summarised the argument: 'The very right to live accrues to us only when we do the duty of the citizenship of the world. From this fundamental statement it is easy enough to define the duties of man and woman and correlate every right to some corresponding duty to be performed. Every other right can be shown to be usurpation hardly worth fighting for' (ibid., Vol. 89, p. 347). The link between specific rights and duties thus becomes a critical part of any policy statement. To use Gandhi's words again: 'Since there never has been any right without a corresponding duty, in my opinion a manifesto is incomplete without emphasizing the necessity of performance of duty and showing what that duty is' (ibid., Vol. 58, p. 76).

The threat that consequentialism poses to rights is thus addressed by the Gandhian method at two levels. To begin with, the method's inclusiveness removes the gap between actions and consequences. This makes the goodness of actions as important as the goodness of consequences. And an action that is good must be sensitive to rights. This sensitivity can, of course, be taken too far if the rights that are being protected actually damage society. The Gandhian method then lays out a second condition that the only rights that can be protected, and should be protected, are those backed by duties. Thus, though Gandhi may not have explicitly stated that the goodness of consequences is sufficient to justify an action, he clearly addressed the issues that would arise if it were to be treated as a sufficient condition.

The principle of judging actions by the goodness of their consequences alone throws up two questions. First, what is to be considered good? Or, to put it differently, what is the morality implicit in the advocacy of an action? And second, what are the options from which the choice has to be made? As Sen puts it: 'In applying consequentialist reasoning to policy issues the task consists essentially of (*a*) determining the outcome morality to be used, and (*b*) identifying the consequences of alternative policies on factors relevant to the chosen outcome morality' (Sen, 1984, p. 295). Both these processes are an essential part of the Gandhian method, but, as the Gandhian method involves an inclusive concept of consequentialism, they are not sufficient. Indeed, the Gandhian method would modify these processes in at least two ways.

First, as the Gandhian method requires the goodness of not just the consequences but of the action itself, considering outcome morality alone would not be enough. The morality involved would need to cover actions as well. In other words, any intervention in the economy would include a moral dimension. As he pointed out in a letter to Rabindranath Tagore, there could be no sharp distinction drawn between economics and ethics (Dasgupta, 1993, pp. 133–34). The extension of the canvas to cover ethics does complicate economic analysis as there could be more than one ethical school at any given point of time and the acceptance of a set of ethical principles could also change over time. But the absence of an absolute morality was not considered a debilitating constraint by Gandhi, as he believed there would be a set of moral principles that could be accepted at any given point of time. In Gandhi's words: 'There is no such thing as absolute morality for all times. But there is a relative morality which is absolute enough for [the] imperfect mortals that we are' (Gandhi, 1958–93, Vol. 71, p. 46).

The treatment of relative morality as absolute reduces the scope for ambiguity in analysis. As far as a particular analysis is concerned there will be no ambiguity about the moral framework that is to be used. But the Gandhian method would acknowledge that this moral framework could be challenged by an alternative framework and that the accepted moral framework could change over time. For instance, Gandhi's approach to moral judgements is often identified with one statement:

> I will give you a talisman. Whenever you are in doubt or when the self becomes too much with you, try the following

expedient: Recall the face of the poorest and the most helpless man whom you may have seen and ask yourself whether the step you contemplate is going to be of any use to him. Will he be able to gain anything by it? Will it restore him to a control over his own life and destiny? In other words, will it lead to ... self-rule for the hungry and also spiritually starved millions of our countrymen? Then you will find your doubts and your self melting away (cited in Easwaran, 1997, p. 150).

This perspective is quite consistent with the 'maximin' approach in welfare economics where 'the goodness of any set of individual utilities must be judged entirely by the value of its least member, that is, by the utility level of the worst-off individual' (Sen, 1984, p. 278). But Gandhi did not reduce the analysis to the absolute, material maximin criterion of welfare economics. He advocated this norm only when there were doubts about the moral value of an action; that is when other criteria were not ethically appealing. And by listing several ways in which the individual's interests could be met, including the spiritual, Gandhi rejected the norm being reduced to a physical increase in the quantity of goods and services available. In other words, even as he claimed that what he was offering was a talisman, he allowed significant room for an individual's judgement.

The Gandhian method can thus operate with different moral systems, and, indeed, allows for a plurality of such systems. This scope for pluralism can influence the acceptability of the Gandhian method itself. Too often Gandhi's ideas are associated with his ascetic lifestyle. There is, in fact, a tendency to believe that the Gandhian method would only be relevant to those who accept a similar ascetic lifestyle. But once we recognise that the method could be equally consistent with a variety of moral frameworks, it gains a wider relevance. It is then quite consistent to use the Gandhian method without subscribing to all of the Mahatma's ascetic objectives.

The second modification that the Gandhian method would bring into the processes involved in a traditional consequentialist approach to choice, is his focus on action. This has two consequences for policy. First, the evaluation of a policy would cover the entire action and not just a theoretical formulation. A policy cannot then be justified on the basis of a theoretical model, even if it is backed by empirical evidence. The analysis would also have to cover the process of implementation of policy. Second, the primacy of action can also alter the role of morality. It is not sufficient to merely evaluate existing options according to a given set of moral norms. The method requires that morality is also used as an active force.

Gandhi's conversion of morality from a given set of norms to an active force was built around the distinction he made between moral, non-moral and immoral actions. An immoral action is one that goes against a given, accepted moral framework. But consistency with a moral framework alone is not enough for an action to qualify as moral in the Gandhian method. Before an action can be considered moral, we must also take into account the intentions of the person carrying out the action as well as the extent of sacrifice involved. It is only when an act that is consistent with a moral framework is also supported by the purity of intention and an element of sacrifice that it would have the force of morality behind it. In the Gandhian framework, only such acts can be considered moral. An act that is consistent with a moral framework but is not backed either by the goodness of intention or by an element of sacrifice will not have the same moral force. Such acts are non-moral.

In Gandhi's words: 'Whether an act is moral or otherwise depends upon the intention of the doer. Two men may have done exactly the same thing; but the act of one may be moral, and that of the other to the contrary. Take, for instance, a man who out of great pity feeds the poor and another who does the same, but with the motive of winning prestige or with some such selfish end. Though the action is the same, the act of the one is moral and that of the other non-moral' (Gandhi, 1958–93, Vol. 6, p. 285). In addition, it was not 'enough for a moral act to have been done with a good intention, but it should have been done without compulsion.... There is no morality in my living a simple and unpretentious life if I have not the means to live otherwise' (ibid., p. 285). It is the purity of intention combined with the sacrifice involved that provides strength to the moral idea as a means of convincing others. Implicit in this distinction between the moral and the non-moral is 'the distinction between the two words, non-moral and immoral' (ibid., p. 285).

Ignoring this distinction can distort, and, in fact, has distorted, the interpretation of the Gandhian method. As Gandhi expected, non-moral actions have not been effective because they do not have the moral edge that is provided either by good intentions or by sacrifice. But without a clear distinction being made between moral, non-moral and immoral actions, non-moral actions are often treated as moral actions. The failure of non-moral actions as an instrument of intervention in the economy or society are then seen as the failure of moral actions. If we restrict the term moral actions to describe only those actions that are backed by both good intentions and sacrifice, their impact on the real world is very much more visible. Gandhians could legitimately claim that Gandhi's use of moral force as an instrument of action did fundamentally alter the relations between pre-Independence India and imperial Britain.

Greater awareness of the distinction between the moral, the non-moral and the immoral would also help ensure that the appropriate concept is chosen depending upon the use to which it is to be put. For instance, when considering the moral basis for deciding whether an action or its consequence is good or not, using Gandhi's strict definition of a moral action would clearly be counterproductive as it could lead to the rejection of worthy actions with desirable consequences. It would also go against Gandhi's contention that his strict definition of moral actions 'is not to say that actions prompted by self-interest are all worthless, but only that to call them moral would detract from the [dignity of the] moral idea' (ibid., p. 286). In other words, Gandhi's strict definition of what is moral is designed to help understand and develop moral force, but when considering the moral basis for deciding whether an action is good or not, a wider definition would be necessary. For the latter purpose, morality would have to include not just what is considered moral but also what is considered non-moral, while excluding what is immoral.

The emphasis on action also influences the approach to options. Rather than merely evaluating the available options, the Gandhian method would also seek to create new options. The active role that the Gandhian method envisages for increasing options is perhaps best seen in Gandhi's strategy for the less privileged. He believed that the best way to empower them was to increase their options. One of the objectives of his campaign for *khadi,* or homespun cloth, was to provide alternative occupations for workers.[2] As Gandhi saw it, the question 'that arises is what are you to do if the employers will not employ you on your own terms. After having respectfully tendered your submission to your employers you should no more think about that submission. But you must set about working for your own livelihood. I have therefore suggested to the mill-hands of Ahmedabad and the railway employees on the Assam-Bengal Railway and the employees of the River Steam Navigation Company that they should always have a supplementary occupation to fall back upon, and the only occupation that thousands upon thousands of our countrymen can usefully occupy themselves in is hand-spinning, carding and weaving' (Gandhi, 1958–93, Vol. 21, p. 133).

As the need for options was not restricted to industrial workers alone, the appeal of khadi also had to be extended to a wider audience. Gandhi was quite clear that the 'mission of *khadi* is not merely to supply the townspeople with fashionable *khadi* that will vie with the mill manufactures and thus like other industries supply a few artisans with employment, but is to become a supplementary industry to agriculture.... In order that it may fulfill this mission, it has to be self-sufficient and its use must spread in the villages' (ibid., Vol. 61, p. 232).

These modifications would alter the process that Sen had outlined for applying consequentialist reasoning to policy issues. In the Gandhian method, this process would consist primarily of (*a*) determining a morality to be used to judge both actions and consequences, (*b*) using this morality as an active instrument to achieve the desired consequences, *(c)* identifying the consequences of alternative policies, and *(d)* working to increase the number of policy options available at any given point of time.

When stated in this form, it should be quite obvious that the Gandhian method cannot function in terms of objective criteria alone. Each of the four steps listed above would involve a subjective dimension. The choice of the relative morality to be used could vary from person to person. Converting moral principles into a force involved, for Gandhi, both sacrifice and the goodness of intentions. Identifying the consequences of specific policies would depend on the knowledge base available at any given point of time. This knowledge too, as we shall see later in this chapter, cannot be a completely objective exercise. And the choice of additional options that can be explored will also include a subjective dimension. This prominent role for the subjective is not accidental, as it is a direct consequence of identifying a role for both the doer and the knower in an action. Dealing with subjectivity is, therefore, an essential element of the Gandhian method.

IMPROVING SUBJECTIVITY

The attitude of the Gandhian method to subjectivity is, in a sense, determined by its inclusiveness. As the method aims at considering all factors affecting an action, it does not have the option of either ignoring the subjective or defining problems in a way that keeps out the subjective. Instead, the method concentrates on improving the quality of subjective judgements. The task of bringing about such an improvement in the quality can be broken down essentially to two elements: first, ensuring that subjective judgements are not influenced by individual or group interests; and second, reducing the risk of a genuine error of judgement.

At the first level, one of the possible misuses of subjectivity would be to allow expediency to influence the formulation and implementation of a policy. Gandhi's main weapon against such expediency was his moral pressure. This pressure may not be significant if morality is seen in individual terms alone.

It would, after all, be clearly idealistic to expect every single individual involved in the formulation and implementation of a policy to personally adopt high moral standards. But Gandhi's use of morality had a social dimension. Gandhi believed 'all morality involves social relations' (Gandhi, 1958–93, Vol. 6, p. 330). It would, therefore, be possible to generate social pressure on individuals less inclined to follow the moral path. And this moral pressure would be greater if the intentions of those exerting the pressure were above board, they were not doing it out of compulsion, and in exerting that pressure an element of sacrifice was involved. To put it in Gandhian terms, moral force could be used to increase the incidence of non-moral actions, thereby reducing the frequency of immoral actions.

Gandhi also reduced the scope for expediency by refusing to accept moral justification for promoting self-interest. We have already seen how his definition of morality explicitly ruled out actions prompted by self-interest. He went on to detect the scope for expediency in theories that suggested that actions prompted by self-interest could lead to a morally superior position in the future. He was thus quick to reject theories based on class struggle. 'If capital is power, so is work. Either power can be used destructively or creatively. Either is dependent on the other. Immediately the worker realises his strength, he is in a position to become a co-sharer with the capitalist instead of remaining his slave. If he aims at becoming the sole earner, he will most likely be killing the hen that lays golden eggs' (ibid., Vol. 45, p. 339).

The inclusiveness of the Gandhian method provides a further safeguard against expediency. The method does not allow any justification for ignoring factors that could influence the consequences of an action. Factors would need to be taken into account even if they are considered minor at that point of time. Gandhi paid a great deal of attention to questions involving the environment long before mainstream policy makers found a prominent place for it.[3] The inclusiveness also does not allow for existing social relations to be divorced from policy making on the grounds that they are undesirable. No matter how much policy makers may dislike differences on the basis of religion, caste or race, they had to be explicitly taken into account as long as they existed in reality. Gandhi clearly rejected the belief that conflict between social groups could be reduced by ignoring the differences between them. Thus, for Gandhi secularism did not mean minimising the role of religion, but providing equal opportunities to all religions.[4] He was even willing to accept caste as long as the inequalities between castes, particularly repugnant practices like untouchability, were removed.[5]

Having rejected all justifications for self-interest dominating the subjective elements of a policy action, Gandhi also recognised the possibility of self-interest subconsciously influencing the choice of a policy action. Gandhi sought to reduce the scope for such unintended bias through the principle of non-attachment. As long as a person was not attached to the consequences of an action, the bias towards one or the other action would be reduced. Gandhi thus emphasised the need to be non-attached not only to the material but also to nonmaterial wants. He thus used a rather austere definition of non-attachment.

> Non attachment means the absence of attachment. Attachment means the desire for a certain fruit. Attachment is implicit in wanting to climb the Himalayas. Climbing the Himalayas when it falls to one's lot is doing it free of attachment (Gandhi, 1958–93, Vol. 45, p. 44).

The severity of the conditions on the person seeking knowledge has contributed to the Gandhian perspective being treated as an idealistic one. Few, if any, living in a modern society will be willing, or even able, to meet the stringent conditions that Gandhi lays down for the ideal person seeking knowledge. But the critical element here is that Gandhi was only defining the ideal. And, as he was fond of pointing out, the ideal could never be realised. The persons seeking knowledge would then necessarily be less than the ideal. But the judgements of those closer to the ideal would be less prompted by self-interest than the judgement of those who did not even attempt to meet this standard. Apart from being a means of improving one's own subjective judgements, an explicit recognition of the role of non-attachment would allow others to judge the extent and direction of the bias in a particular judgement that influences the choice of a policy option. An awareness of the attachment of a policy maker to the consequences of his policy actions would make it easier to understand the kind of distortions that could creep into the policy.

Thus though the Gandhian method works actively to reduce the bias involved in subjective judgements, it clearly does not expect the policy maker to be free of all subjective bias. And even if we assume that all bias, conscious and subconscious, is removed, it is still quite possible that the consequences eventually turn out to be quite different from what was originally anticipated. It is very likely that at least some of those who initially supported either Hitler's fascism or Stalinism in the Soviet Union expected the consequences of their actions to be very different from the way it finally turned out. The Gandhian method thus recognises that error can be minimised but never removed. The inclusiveness of the method ensures that this possibility of error cannot be ignored, however minimal it may appear to be at any given point of time. Gandhi tried to limit the costs of such errors by stressing the means as much as the ends. No matter how attractive the desired consequences may seem, it did not justify an action that was not good in itself. At the same time, the primacy of action in the Gandhian method implies that the possibility of error should not deter action. Once an action is itself good, the uncertainty over the consequences of that action can no longer be used as an excuse for inaction. Indeed, Gandhi insisted 'all that we need to see is that the act is good and is done with a good intention' (Gandhi, 1958–93, Vol. 6, p. 285).

THE CONCEPT OF KNOWLEDGE

The concept of action that Gandhi borrowed from the Bhagvadgita makes knowledge just one component of the totality of action. And Gandhi's consequentialism takes the primacy of action one step further. The need for knowledge was itself to be understood only in terms of its impact on action. As he put it: 'The necessity of knowledge has been accepted for the reason that one may not commit an error in spite of a pure motive' (Gandhi, 1958–93, Vol. 44, p. 223).

Treating knowledge as no more than an instrument to action makes its own demands on the concept of knowledge in the Gandhian method. As action cannot be deferred till perfect knowledge is available, the concept must allow for functioning with less than perfect knowledge. With all factors, including apparently minor ones, needing to be considered when evaluating an action, the concept of knowledge that can support such an evaluation would also have to be inclusive.

In seeking such a concept of knowledge, Gandhi returned to the Bhagvadgita; relying quite heavily on Chapter XIII of the Hindu text. The most striking aspect of the concept of knowledge in the Bhagvadgita is the explicit acknowledgement of the role of the subjective. The very contention that knowledge continuously changes as a result of the interaction between the understanding of the specific and the understanding of the general reflects a belief that the subjective elements of knowledge cannot be ignored. The Gita, in fact, goes further and makes this quite explicit:

> Knowledge of the Field and the knower of the Field, I hold, is true knowledge (cited in Gandhi, 1996, p. 235).

The inclusion of the knower in the concept of knowledge itself does more than merely introduce subjectivity. It defines a role for subjectivity that allows it to coexist with objective facts. When a distinction is made within knowledge between the field and the knower of the field, knowledge does not have to be either entirely subjective or entirely objective. The concept of knowledge that Gandhi borrowed from the Gita allows for the field to have an objective truth even as the knower of the field introduces a subjective interpretation of that truth.

A modernist's objection to this approach would be: How does one know where the field stops and the knower of the field takes over? The inability to provide an unambiguous answer to this question would be a debilitating weakness if such a dividing line was to be defined by objective criteria alone. But once we accept that the subjective forms a part of knowledge, subjective factors must also influence this demarcation. The perception of this dividing line would then vary from person to person, with greater knowledge leading to a more accurate distinction between the field and the knower of the field. In the words of the Gita:

> Those who, with the eyes of knowledge, thus perceive the distinction between the Field and the knower of the Field, ... they attain to Supreme (cited in Gandhi, 1996, p. 241).

Since knowledge is needed to perceive the distinction between the field and the knower of the field, an accurate understanding of this distinction cannot be a precondition for gaining knowledge. Any perception of the field then will always be modified by the subjective perceptions of the knower of the field. And since these perceptions will keep improving with the addition of new knowledge, or what is not known to begin with, it is not possible to know before hand where that knowledge will come from. It is thus essential to include as many elements as possible in the search for knowledge. It is this inclusiveness that is elaborated in the Gita's concept of the field:

> The great elements, Individuation, Reason, the Unmanifest, the ten senses, and the one (mind), and the five spheres of the senses; Desire, dislike, pleasure, pain, association, consciousness, cohesion—this, in sum, is what is called the Field and its modifications (cited in Gandhi, 1996, pp. 235–36).

The inclusiveness of this concept of knowledge increases the number of elements that need to be analysed and hence the number of subjective interpretations that are possible. As each interpretation is less than perfect, there can be no single interpretation that can be advocated to the exclusion of all other interpretations. Pluralism is thus implicit in this concept of knowledge. The Gita, in fact, makes this pluralism explicit in its explanation of the understanding of the self:

> Some through meditation behold the *atman* by themselves in their own self; others by *Sankya Yoga,* and others by *Karma Yoga* (cited in Gandhi, 1996, p. 239).[6]

We have seen that Gandhi himself chose to emphasise *Karma Yoga,* or what other translators of the Gita have called 'the discipline of action' (Johnson, 1994, p. 59).

TRUTH AND FAITH

The demarcation of knowledge between the field and the knower of the field has its implications for the treatment of subjectivity. As the demarcation is itself influenced by subjective judgements, the precise demarcation between objective facts and subjective judgements would vary from person to person as well as over time. Gandhi addressed the blurring of this distinction by first putting the significance of this demarcation in perspective. He recognised that this demarcation could never be perfect. This is implicit in his perception of truth. For Gandhi absolute truth was but an ideal. And like all ideals, absolute truth could also not be realised. 'Euclid has defined a straight line as having no breadth, but no one has yet succeeded in drawing such a line and no one will. Still we can progress in geometry only by postulating such a line. This is true of every ideal' (Gandhi, 1958–93, Vol. 85, p. 266). But given the importance of action in the Gandhian method, the fact that the absolute truth could not be realised was not sufficient reason to stop action. Gandhi addressed this problem by distinguishing between absolute truth and relative truth. The absolute truth for Gandhi 'is total and all-embracing. But it is indescribable.... Other things, therefore, can be true only in a relative sense' (ibid., Vol. 21, pp. 472–73). Since absolute truth was like Euclid's definition of a line, all analysis functioned only with relative truth.

> In our endeavour to approach absolute truth we shall always have to be content with relative truth from time to

time, the relative at each stage being for us as good as the absolute. It can easily be demonstrated that there would be no progress if there was no such confidence in oneself. Of course our language would be one of caution and hesitation if we had any doubt about the correctness of our position (Gandhi, 1958–93, Vol. 49, pp. 478–79).

The willingness to function with relative truth would also influence the demarcation between the subjective and the objective. While this demarcation could not be absolute or perfect, it would be based on relative truth. In other words, the inability to come up with a perfect objectively defined demarcation was not sufficient reason for the demarcation itself to be discarded. Instead, the Gandhian method would be satisfied with a less than perfect demarcation, which includes an element of subjectivity.

The possible adverse consequences of such a less than perfect demarcation are minimised by the inclusiveness of the Gandhian method. Even if an objective fact was mistakenly taken to be subjective, its impact on the final analysis would be relatively limited. The inclusiveness of the method would prevent a fact that was not completely objective from being discarded. Thus Gandhi argued that there is a place not just for reason, but also for faith. But this faith could not become an excuse for ignoring reason. While both reason and faith are integral parts of the Gandhian method, reason always has precedence over faith. As Gandhi saw it, 'Faith has no place in a sphere in which we can exercise our reason. Faith has meaning only in relation to what is above reason' (ibid., Vol. 31, p. 24).

A major advantage of the Gandhian method going beyond reason is that it can then internalise the incompleteness of knowledge. Rather than fearing the uncertainties resulting from less than perfect knowledge, it considers them an unavoidable part of the analysis that precedes the choice of an appropriate action. It thus provides a specific place for the problems arising out of incomplete knowledge, instead of either ignoring them or using them as an excuse for going against the rational. Any action must then be evaluated on the basis of a wider knowledge base that includes not just the rational but also faith.

EVALUATING AN ACTION

A method that provides as explicit and significant a role for subjectivity as the Gandhian one does, runs a risk of encouraging anarchism. The safeguards the method develops to prevent subjectivity degenerating into expediency are focused on the individual. Even when moral pressure is built up at the social level, the target of the pressure is the individual. And it is not always easy to distinguish between an individual who is subjecting himself to a moral code and one who is not. Equally significantly, morality cannot prevent unintended errors in subjective judgements. Thus while the incorporation of subjectivity provides the Gandhian method with much needed inclusiveness, it also brings with it the risk of disguising expediency or hiding inefficient subjective judgements. In order to overcome this risk, any action that is advocated on the basis of the Gandhian method must be subject to an objective evaluation.

The objective test of actions in the Gandhian method is built into its principle of consequentialism. The validity or otherwise of an action would be determined by the goodness of both the action itself and its consequences. Given a moral system to determine what is good, it should be possible to evaluate every action once the consequences are known. But an action could have more than one consequence, thereby creating the possibility of an action generating both positive and negative consequences. An action could then be justified by stressing the positive consequences and ignoring the negative ones. In order to guard against this immunising stratagem, it is necessary to add the condition that when an action is chosen, the moral framework and the relative priorities of different possible consequences should be specified. The validity of an action could then be decided on the basis of how its consequences match the desired consequences listed at the outset.

While such a test of history would evaluate a policy maker's actions after they have been implemented, it would not be useful to choose between conflicting policy options before they are implemented. The test of history may be an effective ex post evaluation of an action, but policy makers require a method of evaluation that is ex ante. It is here that the Gandhian method can benefit from the work of others who recognised the need to look for knowledge beyond narrowly defined concepts of science. Keynes had used probability to understand issues on which there could only be partial belief. But even while Keynes stepped outside the bounds of conventional rationality, the effort was to bring the new areas within the realm of rationality. Keynes believed that 'the theory of probability is logical ... because it is concerned with the degree of belief which it is rational to entertain in given conditions, and not merely with the actual beliefs of particular individuals, which may or may not be rational' (Keynes, 1973, p. 4). Gandhi clearly would not have been as keen on restricting the analysis to the rational alone. But even in his broader framework, the approach Keynes used to deal with partial belief can be useful.

Keynes's treatise on probability is now recognised to have had its flaws. As Braithwaite pointed out in 1973 in a foreword to a later edition of the treatise: 'It is the essence of Keynes's theory that is alive today; the detailed way in which he worked it out has not survived' (Braithwaite, 1973, p. xvi). The problem was that Keynes 'takes a logical probability-relationship between two propositions as fundamental to his explanation of rational partial belief, and he maintains that in suitable cases this relationship can be perceived, directly recognised, intuited.... Most present-day logicians would be chary of using such verbs as "perceive" to describe knowledge of logical consequence relationships.... They would be even more chary of claiming to perceive probability relationships' (ibid., p. xix). But these technical flaws cannot be a case against the argument that the process of gaining knowledge extends beyond narrowly defined boundaries of rationality.

The way later interpreters of Keynes have sought to preserve the essence of the treatise even as they abandoned the details would have pleased Gandhi. This was done by shifting the focus from the probability relationship to the consequences of that probability, that is, the degree of belief. As Braithwaite puts it:

> Many of those today who think about the logic of partial belief would not start with a probability relationship and take a degree of belief as being justified by knowledge that a probability relation holds, but would start with the degree of belief and consider what conditions this must satisfy in order to be regarded as one which a rational man would have under given circumstances. To start this way requires a notion of degrees of belief which is independent of considerations of rationality, and this was provided by F.P. Ramsey in a paper of 1926 written deliberately as a constructive criticism of Keynes's view. Ramsey proposed to measure the degree of belief in a proposition p which a particular man has at a particular time by the rate at which he would be prepared to bet upon p being true, which is to say that a belief of degree q (with $0 \leq q \leq 1$) if the man is prepared to a proportion q of one unit of value (but no more) for the right to receive one unit of value if p is true but nothing if p is false. Degrees of belief when measured in this way will be called (following Rudolf Carnap) betting quotients: A betting quotient measures a man's actual partial belief at a point of time, and in no way depends on whether or not the man has a good reason for holding a partial belief of that degree. To confine the partial belief to being one which is rational is effected by imposing appropriate restrictions upon the betting quotients (Braithwaite, 1975, pp. 240–41).

The use of betting quotients to estimate the degree of belief is consistent with some essential elements of the Gandhian method. It reflects several aspects of Gandhi's concept of knowledge. By trying to estimate a degree of belief, it acknowledges that we are functioning with relative truth rather than absolute truth. As betting quotients are estimated by each individual, they also implicitly recognise that knowledge involves not only knowing the field, but also the person trying to know. Where the Gandhian method would have differed was on the need to confine betting quotients to the rational. If knowledge involved going beyond the rational, then betting quotients should be based on both reason and faith. When faith influences decisions made by an otherwise rational mind, it cannot be ignored.

Such a comprehensive betting quotient can be useful in evaluating the quality of judgements that are being made. A comparison between betting quotients on the consequences of an action before it is taken and the actual consequences of that action will provide an indicator of the quality of an individual's judgements and hence an indicator of the seriousness with which an individual's predictions of the consequences of future actions should be treated.

The main strength of such a test is that it evaluates a comprehensive justification for an action which includes theories and judgements. But it must be emphasised that this test does not provide an evaluation of individual theories or judgements within a comprehensive whole. Even when the overall picture is proved to be valid by history, it could well be that the errors of one theory or judgement are offset by the errors of another theory or judgement within the overall package. For instance, an economist may argue in a particular situation that the impact of an increase in money supply on prices would be zero because supply would rise to meet the additional demand. And in the course of time he is proved to be right in the sense that money supply does increase and there is no change in the price level. But this could have been the result of the increase in money supply being absorbed by higher savings so that there is no impact on demand. The fact that the overall prediction made by the economist has come true does not then justify his individual theories and judgements.

In addition to evaluating an action as a whole, therefore, it is necessary to also test individual elements of that action. In testing these individual elements, betting quotients would be less useful. It may not be difficult to come up with a betting quotient, but what is it to be compared with? As any real situation is the result of the combination of a variety of factors, it would be necessary to isolate each factor. We could use statistical techniques to isolate each factor. But the quality of this isolation would vary from situation to situation. The relationship between demand, supply and price would, normally, be easier to isolate from the rest of the economy than, say, the statement of a less important political leader on the stock markets. Where there is no perfect objective means of isolating an element from the whole, there is scope for subjectivity. And if the perception of reality is itself subjective, it cannot be used as a standard against which to evaluate other subjective judgements.

In dealing with the elements of a situation we would then have to fall back on other more precise objective systems that do not have room for subjectivity. The results of such scientific analysis would gain precedence over other conjectures. But the method would explicitly recognise that these objective tests do not provide the whole story. It would then demand that the subjective dimensions of the analysis be explicitly stated and efforts made to improve the quality of this subjectivity. It would also recognise that the very demarcation between the objective and the subjective would itself involve an element of subjectivity.

In order to get a clearer picture of how the method would work in practice, let us consider a situation, like the one that existed in mainstream economics at the end of the twentieth century, where it is widely believed that a proposition that passes the test prescribed by falsification is scientific. The Gandhian method would then begin by considering all propositions that pass the test prescribed by falsification to be the relative truth. The precise degree of rigour that is required in the test will be subjectively determined. In a statistical test this would take the form of defining an acceptable level of significance. This subjective decision will act as the precise demarcation between the objective and the subjective. All the propositions that are considered subjective will then be kept in the realm of faith. They will only re-enter the picture if there is no objective explanation for a phenomenon. Taken together this exercise should generate a betting quotient to evaluate a particular action.

The essence of the Gandhian method thus lies not in rejecting science, but in recognising the precise role that science plays in the economy and society as a whole. Scientific statements that are consistent with the relative truth prevailing at any point of time get precedence over other contentions. But the inability to come up with a scientifically proved analysis of a particular relationship can never be an excuse for inaction. Instead, in these areas dominated by faith, an effort must be made to improve the quality of subjective judgements.

NOTES

1. This ancient Hindu religious text has been subject to a variety of translations and interpretations. Our interest here is, of course, only in Gandhi's interpretation. All quotations from the Bhagvadgita are also as translated by Gandhi and published in Gandhi (1996).
2. Over the years, the symbolic dimension of the campaign for khadi has tended to overwhelm its other dimensions. Khadi emerged as a political uniform in post-Independence India, particularly for members of the Congress Party. In the process the economic logic behind the campaign for khadi has not received much attention.
3. Gandhi provided a significant role for environmental issues in the Indian national movement. As Gadgil and Guha point out, 'Gandhi's visit to Cudappah in south-eastern India in September 1921 was widely hailed as an opportunity to get the forest laws abolished' (Gadgil and Guha, 1993, p. 162).
4. Gandhi was, in fact, a strong opponent of the efforts to separate religion from politics, arguing that such a separation would remove the spiritual dimension of politics.
5. For an account of Gandhi's views on caste, see Dalton (1998, pp. 49–58).
6. Both the *sankya yoga* and the *karma yoga* are subjects of extensive discourse in Hindu philosophy. To attempt a summary of these concepts in a footnote would be foolhardy. But as a pointer to these concepts it could be said that *karma yoga* refers to action and the Sankya theory 'teaches that material nature ... is a continuous process manifested in the dynamic interaction of three inextricably intertwined constituents, which are respectively pure, passionate and dark. Of these, the pure constituent represents the principles of knowledge and freedom from pollution, the passionate those of activity and greed, the dark those of inertia and ignorance' (Johnson, 1994, pp. 83–84).

3

Economic Action

In developing a Gandhian framework of an economy, the first challenge is to come to terms with the inclusiveness of the method. As the method postulates that all the consequences of an action, large and small, must be considered, it requires understanding a diverse set of relationships between actions and consequences. These relationships range from the impact of demand on the price a firm charges for one of its products to the relationship between the environment and the long-term global availability of natural resources; from the most minute microeconomic relationship to global phenomena. These diverse relationships are also intertwined in a variety of ways. The action of one action-consequence relationship can deeply influence the action of another action-consequence relationship. Reducing costs may be the action prescribed for the consequence of raising profits. But reduced buying by the company would alter the conditions its suppliers face. These interlinked action-consequence relationships get further complicated when an action has unintended consequences. Careless cost control, for instance, can end up crippling a company's critical activities. And there could be actions with an economic impact that are beyond the control of those in charge of the economy. The impact of monsoons on agricultural production or the effect of market failure on the returns to a farmer may be predictable, but still not preventable. The Gandhian method thus visualises the economy as a maze of action-consequence relationships that influence each other, that are not always predictable, and over which it is not always possible to extend the desired degree of control.

Viewing the economy as a maze of action-consequence relationships has at least three implications for the method of understanding the economy. First, it rules out reducing any situation to a grand theory. The development of a grand theory to determine all action-consequence relationships is severely constrained by the sheer volume of the task. Inclusiveness demands that the analysis is not confined to a few core factors, but takes into account other factors that may appear, at first glance, to be relatively minor. A theory must then explain a situation in all its detail. Even if the difficulties involved in developing such a comprehensive theory to understand a particular situation are overcome, there would remain doubts about its value in other situations. For such a comprehensive theory to explain more than one situation in every detail, the situations must be identical. Such identical situations, if they ever do occur, will be extremely rare. What is more likely is that a specific action-consequence relationship may hold in more than one situation. But the precise manner in which that relationship influences the overall picture would vary from situation to situation. An economy that retains a significant barter component, for instance, would be less sensitive to changes in money supply than an advanced market economy. Even if we focus on a single economy, the role a particular action-consequence relationship plays could vary over time. To continue with the example of monetary policy in an advanced economy, the impact of an increase in money supply also depends on whether there are other constraints on production. When production is constrained, a marginal increase in money supply may have an immediate and substantial impact on prices. The impact would be much less if the extra demand generated by the increased money supply is met with greater production. The Gandhian method's insistence on an inclusive detailed analysis of every situation thus makes it difficult to be satisfied with any single theory. As Gandhi put it, it 'is not possible to enunciate one grand principle and leave the rest to follow of itself (Gandhi, 1958–93, Vol. 88, p. 59).

The second implication of viewing the economy as a maze of relationships is for the role of abstraction. The inclusive method is quite consistent with abstraction. It recognises that abstraction is useful, and sometimes essential, to understand a specific action-consequence relationship. Isolating a relationship from the large number of other relationships that influence it, and are influenced by it, helps gain a clearer, more rigorous, view of that relationship. At the same time, inclusiveness militates against reducing reality to a single theory, no matter how sophisticated that theory may be. In other words, individual relationships have to be understood in the abstract, but they must then be put back into the maze that is the real economy. Needless to say, the way a relationship operates in the abstract need not be the same as its operation in the midst of its interaction with a large number of other factors. When seen in isolation, an increase in money supply will always exert an upward pressure on prices. But in the real economy this upward pressure could be offset by factors like increased production or the removal of other supply bottlenecks. In other words, the abstract model is essential for a rigorous analysis, but it cannot be treated as an approximation to reality.

This does not in any way diminish the importance of abstraction. As we shall see a little later, Gandhi frequently abstracted from reality to develop concepts like *Swadeshi* and Trusteeship. But these, and other, abstract concepts were not meant to be approximations to reality. Instead, they were expected to play other very critical roles. They would help understand specific relationships without the distorting influence of other factors that come into play in reality. The understanding of reality would then be based on putting together a set of abstract action-consequence relationships. It is this understanding that would have to approximate to reality and not each action-consequence relationship. To return to our example of money supply and prices, what needs to approximate to reality is not the relationship between money supply and prices alone, but the overall assessment of the situation. In addition, Gandhi also used abstraction to define an ideal. As he was not burdened by the need for his abstractions to approximate to reality, he could define an abstract ideal. These ideals were often not attainable. But they provided a perfect model towards which it was desirable to move. The abstract ideal in the Gandhian method thus differs from the popular perception of a model. It is not expected to be an approximation to reality and it prescribes what should be and not necessarily what is.

A third implication of treating the economy as a maze of interconnected action-consequence relationships is more fundamental. When the economy is viewed as a single homogenous unit, the emphasis is on arriving at a theory that explains the functioning of that unit. Facts that do not fit into that theory are believed to be exceptions that can be ignored. But if the economy is a maze of inter-connected relationships, the precise relationship between an action and a consequence would keep changing both across regions and over time. A theory that works very well in one place at one point of time need not be very useful in explaining the situation in another place or at another point of time. Money supply may be the cause of inflation in an economy with excess liquidity. But it will not be the most relevant factor when inflation is caused by supply bottlenecks. In understanding an economic situation, therefore, it becomes necessary to pick the appropriate theory for that specific relationship in a particular place at a particular point of time. In other words, the problem is now one of choice. The emphasis in understanding an economy shifts from seeking the theory at the core of the economy to choosing the appropriate theory to explain each specific element of a particular situation.

Using the Gandhian method to understand the complex maze of action-consequence relationships that constitute the economy, in fact, involves a series of choices. The desirable consequences for which policies need to be formulated must first be chosen. It is then necessary to identify the policy options that can achieve these desirable consequences. The exercise would involve choosing the appropriate model for each specific relationship. These models must then be put together to form the different options. The choice of the option would then reflect judgements about how the models interact with each other in a given situation.

CHOICE OF OBJECTIVES

The consequentialism of the Gandhian method makes it necessary to begin the policy-making exercise by identifying desirable consequences. The choice of what is desirable is based on a morality. It is this morality that allows us to decide which consequences are desirable and which are not. And except in the rare cases when there is complete unanimity in a society over the morality involved, there would be more than one morality acceptable at any given point of time. This absence of unanimity is anticipated by the Gandhian method, as it recognises the need to function with relative morality. To the extent that there may be more than one relative morality in a society at a given point of time, the pluralism of the Gandhian method is built into the choice of desirable consequences. The ability to function with a variety of relative moralities must not give the impression of the Gandhian method supporting complete relativism. It is not as if any morality goes. The choice of moral system influences the acceptability of an action based on it. The more appealing a moral system, the greater are the chances of an action based on it gaining wide acceptance.

Once the moral system is explicitly stated, there are two other issues that need to be addressed before we can choose the desired consequences. First, should the focus of the policy maker be on individuals or groups; that is, should he be concerned with the individual or with castes, classes, or any other groups? And second, when there is a conflict of interests between different individuals or groups, how should they be resolved?

The answer the Gandhian method provides to the first question is: the individual. Gandhi was convinced this had to be the case since 'ultimately it is the individual who is the unit' (Gandhi, 1958–93, Vol. 85, pp. 32–33); 'if the individual ceases to count, what is left of society?' (ibid., Vol. 73, p. 93). The focus of policy making thus had to be on the final consequences for individuals.

But the individual is not an island. He or she interacts with other individuals in a society. As Gandhi put it, 'Love, kindness, generosity and other qualities can be manifested only in relation to others' (Gandhi, 1958–93, Vol. 6, p. 330). The protection of the interests of one individual must then be seen in the context of the rights of all other individuals. The comprehensive protection of the rights of all individuals would not be possible if in the process of supporting the interests of one individual the interests of others were hurt. 'Unrestricted individualism is the law of the beast of the jungle…. Willing submission to social restraint for the sake of the well-being of the whole society enriches both the individual and the society of which one is a member' (ibid., Vol. 69, p. 258). All consequences, therefore, had to be judged in terms of their impact on individuals operating within society.

It is, of course, impossible for each individual to interact with every other individual in human society. Even if technology made it physically possible to do so, an individual would not have the time, or even the inclination, to deal continuously with every other individual in the world. Individuals would prefer interacting with those who make a difference to their own interests. Thus, if not out of physical necessity, at least due to personal inclination, individuals tend to form groups. These groups may be formed on the basis of a shared nationality, a shared economic interest, a shared social background or a shared whatever. There is thus a natural tendency towards the creation of groups whether it is on the basis of caste, class, nationality, language, or any other criterion. Indeed, individuals may belong to more than one group. We could easily have an upper-caste individual who is economically a part of the poorest class. It is then extremely unlikely that a society would emerge that is completely free of groups. Even if a classless or a casteless society is created, it would only be a prelude to the creation of new social groups.

Accepting the inevitability of social groups has its own implications for the role of the individual. If it was possible not to have any groups at all, we could define ideals in terms of a caste-less, classless, or any-other-groupless society. But when social groups are inevitable, the focus must be on ensuring that the individual is not overwhelmed by the pressures faced by the group he or she happens to belong to. In particular, the fact that an individual belongs to a particular caste or class must not be a disadvantage. This could be ensured through equality between castes, classes, nationalities, etc. It is thus not really coincidental that Gandhi concentrated on trying to bring about equality between castes rather than focusing entirely on removing caste. Again, rather than arguing that a classless society was possible, he argued for cooperation between classes. The Gandhian method's focus on the individual thus does not imply that other groups do not exist, or even that they should not exist. All that the Gandhian method would like to see is that the individual is not treated as a faceless entity in a group.

Having decided that the focus, when identifying the consequences, must be on the individual, we come to the second question that needs to be answered before we choose the desired consequences. How do we resolve conflicts of interests between different individuals? Gandhi's vision of a society was one based on cooperation between individuals. Such cooperation would be easiest in the case of a consensus born out of a unanimity of views. But waiting for a consensus based on unanimity would have little practical value in a large and diverse society, where conflicts of interests and perceptions are inevitable. For consensus to be a practical instrument, it has to be used even when there is a conflict. In other words, consensus has to also be a means of resolving a conflict. As this consensus is not based on unanimity of views, it has to involve a compromise. The details of such a compromise would be worked out through a process of bargaining. And in this bargaining process each individual would be able to use moral pressure. This view of bargained consensus is reflected in Gandhi's insistence that 'non-co-operation... is a prelude to co-operation' (Gandhi, 1958–93, Vol. 41, p. 379).

Several things could obviously go wrong in arriving at a bargained consensus. The final result could reflect the relative bargaining strength of each group rather than a fair solution. And a process of unrestrained bargaining through the creation of pressure could disrupt society itself. Each group could quite simply use all kinds of pressure tactics to a point where the social system itself breaks down. Gandhi sought to reduce these risks primarily through three measures.

First, he ruled out the violent disruption of the bargaining process by emphasising non-violence. Non-violence had to be the norm not just in the physical sense, but also in the realm of the intellectual. There had to be a willingness to listen to alternative points of view. Tolerance to alternative points of view and non-violence are thus essential parts of the Gandhian method. Any compromise on this score would lead to the bargaining process becoming socially disruptive. A deeply divided and angry society would make bargaining impossible. The Gandhian method would then not be in a position to complete even the first step of identifying the desired consequences for a society.

The second measure to reduce the possibility of an unfair bargained consensus is the empowerment of the weaker groups. Ideally, if all groups had equal strength and awareness of their interests, it would be easier to come up with a consensus that does not treat any single group unfairly. But in reality, groups are unequal. The inequality need not be in economic terms alone. Some groups are numerically larger than others. The social status enjoyed by different groups also tends to differ. The bargained consensus would then be more fair if it were achieved after the empowerment of the weaker groups. And this process of empowerment would have different dimensions to it. In order to overcome numerical inequalities, limits would have to be placed on the dominance of the majority. The interests of the minorities would have to be protected. Economic inequalities would have to be offset by improving the bargaining power of the poor. This could be achieved by increasing the economic options open to them. It is not sufficient to merely evaluate the options available. There is a need to develop new options. This could take the form of developing new industries that offer options to the weaker sections. In Gandhi's time this took the form of economic activity based on khadi. Contemporary options could include offering agricultural labour income-earning opportunities outside agriculture. Options could also exist in other less tangible forms. At a time when economic analysis was dominated by efforts to increase production to meet growing demand, Gandhi argued that controlling wants was also an option. Gandhi did not believe that merely increasing the availability of commodities would be able to satisfy human wants. As he saw it, 'The mind is a restless bird; the more it gets the more it wants, and still remains unsatisfied' (Gandhi, 1958–93, Vol. 10, p. 37). Satisfaction, therefore, is dependent not just on increasing the availability of commodities, but also on ensuring that the individuals' demands are within achievable limits. As long as the demands are material, these limits can be broadly defined at any point of time, depending on factors like technology and the access of the individual to resources. But there is nothing final about these limits. The limits in terms of the availability of material goods could themselves be extended through conservation and technological change. And the overall limits could be extended even further if the demands are not confined to the material. This could be achieved by stressing the spiritual requirements of an individual. If an individual's search for greater satisfaction takes a spiritual form, his demand for material goods could stabilise or even decrease. Once the satisfaction from spiritual aspects is taken into account, it becomes easier to limit an individual's demand for material goods. In the Gandhian method, therefore, it is not just the supply of goods and services that has to be improved, but the nature and magnitude of individual demand also need to be controlled by the individual himself. The creation of such control would empower even those who are materially less endowed as they would develop non-material options.

The social dimension of empowerment calls for a two-pronged approach. At one level it will require increasing the awareness of the socially weaker groups. They would need to be made aware of their rights, so that they do not hesitate to identify and benefit from specific opportunities. But if this awareness is increased in isolation, it will only lead to conflict, contributing to a breakdown of the system of bargained consensus. It is thus essential that the increased awareness of the weaker sections is accompanied by the sensitisation of the dominant sections. As long as the dominant sections of society accept a more equal social role for the weaker sections, the process of social empowerment will be smooth or at least less likely to disrupt the process of arriving at a bargained consensus.

Sustained empowerment of the weak need not, however, be an unmixed blessing. The support for the oppressed in one situation could, over time, create new inequalities. Those who are oppressed today may be empowered tomorrow and become the new oppressors the day after. The third essential requirement for effective bargaining in the Gandhian method is thus the creation of a method of fairness. Economics for Gandhi was thus inextricably linked to ethics. And one of the more innovative concepts that Gandhi developed to explore the link between ethics and economics was Trusteeship.

TRUSTEESHIP

The system of fairness that Gandhi sought to develop was built around non-attachment. This was based on the principle that a person was more likely to be fair if he was not attached to the consequences of the action he chose. Gandhi sought to institutionalise this perception of non-attachment as fairness through his concept of Trusteeship.

Gandhi's concept of Trusteeship is built on the difference between an individual and the resources he commands. This distinction is easily recognised in the case of the capitalist and his capital. But it is possible to extend this distinction to other inputs. A similar distinction can be made in the case of labour as well. Labour, for Gandhi, was 'as much capital as metal' (Gandhi, 1958–93, Vol. 59, p. 140). In other words, Gandhi was making a distinction similar to the one that Marxists make between labour and labour power. Where Gandhi went a step further was in insisting that this conceptual distinction could be translated into practice, if the owner of each factor of production acted as no more than a trustee of that factor of production. As he saw it, a 'trustee is one who discharges the obligations of his trust faithfully and in the best interests of his wards' (Gandhi, 1958–93, Vol. 90, p. 521). And the labourer could be the trustee of his labour just as much as the capitalist could be the trustee of his capital. Gandhi argued that 'workers instead of regarding themselves as enemies of the rich, or regarding the rich as their natural enemies, should hold their labour in trust for those who are in need of it' (ibid., Vol. 59, p. 140).

This concept of Trusteeship has two distinct dimensions to it. The first is the definition of fairness that is implied in the concept, and the second the question of its practicality. The fairness is based on the belief that if each individual is non-attached to the economic resources he commands, the judgements he makes would not be determined solely by his economic interests. He would then be as fair in his judgements as was possible given the knowledge available to him. And the results of a bargaining process where everyone was not attached to the resources at their command would be fair. The claims of Trusteeship to fairness would thus appear to be well founded. It is the second aspect—the question of practicality—that has attracted greater scepticism. Is it possible for an individual to be completely non-attached to the resources at his command? Gandhi was quite aware of the difficulties in converting Trusteeship into a regular practice. He recognised that getting owners of a factor of production to restrict their role solely to that of a trustee would not be easy. But he did not believe that Trusteeship would be of value only in its purest form. He argued that any movement in that direction would be a step forward. 'Absolute trusteeship is an abstraction like Euclid's definition of a point, and is equally unattainable. But if we strive for it, we shall be able to go further in realising a state of equality on earth than by any other method' (ibid., p. 318).

The combination of non-violence and tolerance, empowerment through options, and fairness through non-attachment and Trusteeship would thus help resolve conflicts between individuals when choosing the desired consequences. It should then be possible to arrive at a set of prioritised desired consequences.

SWADESHI

When putting together a bargained consensus on the choice of desired consequences, we come up against a major practical difficulty. The inclusiveness of the method requires that we take into account all consequences for everybody in the world. The importance of such a universal view of consequences for the Gandhian method is reflected in Gandhi's own actions. When he called for a boycott of foreign goods at the height of the Indian national movement, he used the first opportunity available to justify this action to the workers in Lancashire whose jobs were threatened by the boycott.[1] More significantly, one of the reasons cited for their crime by those involved in the assassination of Gandhi was the pressure that he exerted on the Indian government to pay a substantial amount that was due to Pakistan.[2]

But implementing a universal bargained consensus would clearly be impossible. There would be consequences that are not known at the time when an action is taken, and some of these consequences may not be known simply because they occur at too remote a place from where the action is being decided upon. These practical difficulties of consequentialism have been recognised in welfare economics (Sen, 1984, p. 295). And these difficulties cannot simply be assumed away in the Gandhian method as the focus of the method on action makes practical difficulties as important as theoretical ones. There is then a need to develop theoretical concepts that address the practical problems caused by the inclusiveness of the method. The concept Gandhi developed to meet this challenge was Swadeshi.

The term Swadeshi has been open to diverse interpretations, including a view that it is another name for protectionism. But as is evident from the preceding discussion on inclusive consequentialism, protectionism is quite inconsistent with the Gandhian method. Protectionism focuses entirely on a group within a national boundary, while the Gandhian method requires the consequences on people outside national boundaries to also be taken into account.

Gandhi's concept of Swadeshi was very different. He defined a universal concept of Swadeshi that was not confined to national boundaries. In 1916, Gandhi announced, 'After much thinking, I have arrived at a definition of swadeshi that perhaps best illustrates my meaning. Swadeshi is that spirit in us which restricts us to the use and service of our immediate surroundings to the exclusion of the more remote' (Gandhi, 1958–93, Vol. 13, p. 219).

This definition implies that when choosing the desired consequences for which an action is to be formulated, the focus must be on the immediate surroundings alone. This would remove several of the practical difficulties involved in arriving at a set of desirable consequences through a bargained consensus. By restricting the focus on the local it should be easier to identify the major consequences that matter. The bargained consensus would also be more practical as it would involve only local groups.

This localised focus may appear contradictory to Gandhi's inclusive view of consequentialism. But that is only if we do not recognise the distinction between the desired consequences and the other consequences of an action. While the desired consequences are the consequences in pursuit of which an action is formulated, the action could also generate other consequences, both positive and negative. The concept of Swadeshi demands only that the desired consequences are kept local. When the actions that can achieve these consequences are analysed, the inclusiveness of the Gandhian method would come into play. This inclusiveness makes it necessary to take into account all the non-local consequences of an action. True, it may not always be possible to know all the consequences of an action outside the local economy. But an effort must be made to understand as many of these non-local consequences as possible. The desired local consequences must then be evaluated in the context of the consequences elsewhere. If the adverse consequences elsewhere are seen to be less significant than the desired consequences in the immediate surroundings, the action would be justified. The decision to boycott foreign cloth as a part of the Indian national movement was thus considered just, though efforts had to be made to convince the workers in Lancashire that this was the case. But this does not mean that the benefit of the immediate surroundings will always be preferable to consequences elsewhere. In situations where the non-local consequences outweigh the local, the non-local consequences must get precedence.

Deciding upon the relative merits of local and non-local consequences introduces another conflict of interest. If the bargained consensus is among local groups, they will tend to favour local interests over the non-local. Despite Gandhi's stature, his insistence that India should pay Pakistan what he believed was due to the latter generated considerable resentment within India.[3] The resolution of this conflict will require a bargained consensus between the local economy and the other economies that feel the consequences of a local action. A local economy on a river basin may be submerged by a large hydel project. The benefits of this project for the national economy may be far in excess of the costs to the local economy. But those dependent on the local economy may well believe that the compensation offered to them is inadequate. The Gandhian method would attempt to arrive at a bargained consensus between the local economy and the economies that benefit from the large hydel project. And this bargained consensus would achieve the best results if the three conditions of tolerance, empowerment and fairness are met. Representatives of one local economy would need to be tolerant of the views of the representatives of other local economies. Each local economy must be empowered to be able to protect its own interests. And it should be possible to identify a fair solution using the principle of non-attachment.

The Swadeshi principle would thus involve a series of actions based on bargained consensus. Once it is clear that the local desired consequences and the actions to achieve them have consequences outside the local economy, other interests enter the picture. This calls for another bargained consensus between the local economy and the other affected economies. In arriving at this consensus new options can be considered. The exercise of these options could, in turn, affect other economies. This would bring fresh interests into the picture, requiring another bargained consensus between the first set of economies and the ones that are now affected. And so on.

When seen as a sequence of actions based on bargained consensus, Swadeshi cannot be defined in terms of a single unit whether it is the local economy, the national economy, or a regional bloc. Instead, it is a series of links from the local economy right up to the global economy. The relevant immediate surroundings at each point will then keep changing. For a rural individual, the immediate economic surroundings may be the village economy. If the actions in that village have an effect on other villages in the vicinity, there would need to be a bargained consensus among the villages. The immediate surroundings in the new context would be extended to cover the group of villages. The immediate surroundings for the group of villages in turn would be the next level of aggregation, say a district or a state; for the state it would be the country; and for the country, in a contemporary situation, it would be the regional bloc.

This example must not give the impression that each level of aggregation in the Swadeshi sequence is necessarily defined in geographical terms alone. There are issues for which the immediate surroundings would vary between neighbours. There may not be too great a geographical distance between the resident of a mansion and the person dwelling in a hutment just outside the walls of the mansion. But on several economic issues, the immediate surroundings of the hutment dweller may be people of his class elsewhere, rather than the resident of the neighbouring mansion. The relevant immediate surroundings thus vary from issue to issue.

This flexibility built into the concept of Swadeshi creates two demands on the policy maker who seeks to use the Gandhian method. First, it demands particular attention to the identification of the appropriate unit of analysis. The Gandhian method is very sensitive to the fact that the choice of an inappropriate unit of analysis could completely distort the understanding of a particular situation. It recognises that what holds for individuals may not hold for society as a whole. To take an obvious, simple, example, a person standing in a rear row of a crowd viewing a procession may be able to get a better view by standing on his toes. But if everyone stands on their toes, this benefit would be nullified. Standing on one's toes may be useful for an individual but is of little use for the group as a whole. There are several economic equivalents of this example. To cite a popular one, when an individual saves more it might give him a greater sense of economic well-being. But if everyone in the economy steps up their savings, it will result in a fall in demand and hence in a lower income, thereby reducing the sense of economic well-being. The appropriate unit need not also always be obvious. Sometimes a local phenomenon may be best understood through an analysis of global phenomena. For instance, a small grower in a remote district of an underdeveloped country could be affected by changes in the world prices of the commodity he grows. And these factors could have nothing to do with conditions in the local economy. Coffee prices in the small district of Kodagu in southern India have been known to be affected by a frost in Brazil. Effective evaluation of the consequences for the individual must then necessarily put together analyses made at different levels. If there is still a fallacy of composition, it would then be the result of choosing an inappropriate unit rather than the failure of the method itself.

The second demand made on the policy maker is that the policy implementing mechanism is flexible enough to meet the demands of Swadeshi. Take the example of a human settlement on the banks of a river. Some issues, such as making the most efficient use of the water, are perhaps best analysed for the river basin as a whole. But for the same community, other issues, like the performance of the teacher at the local school, are best analysed at the local level. And the impact of international trends on the prices of the crops they produce are best analysed at the global level. The levels of aggregation too would, ideally, vary from issue to issue. On policies related to river waters, the levels of aggregation would ideally move from the local economy to the river basin, which could cut across several states. For literacy, on the other hand, the ideal would be to move from the village to the larger region speaking the same language.

Decentralisation in the Gandhian method cannot then be seen in absolute terms. What is needed is that the policy maker addresses each issue at the most decentralised level appropriate for that issue and then proceeds to aggregate the local economies into the specific categories appropriate to that issue. In some cases, the most decentralised level possible may well be the national or even the global economy. Gandhi was, in fact, quite explicit in his view that there was 'no incompatibility in the idea of decentralising, to the greatest extent possible, all industries and crafts, economically profitable in the villages of India, and centralising the key and vital large industries required for India considered as a whole' (Gandhi, 1958–93, Vol. 80, p. 352).

Gandhi's concept of Swadeshi together with the focus on the individual thus provides a link between the inclusiveness of his consequentialism and the fact that, in practical terms, the urge to action tends to be local. Swadeshi is thus essential to the Gandhian method of arriving at a set of desirable consequences. And it is these consequences that determine the actions that are to be considered and the policy options that emerge from them.

CHOICE OF ACTIONS

The choice of the appropriate action to achieve a particular desired consequence will require considering all possible options. A search that is restricted to a few options may ignore opportunities, as well as risks, that exist in a particular situation. For instance, containing inflation is sometimes seen as entirely a matter of controlling money supply. This ignores the potential that might exist in some situations for controlling prices through the removal of local supply bottlenecks. Before choosing an option, therefore, it is important that all possible options are considered. This would require the effective development of each of the options, so that a fair comparison is possible. Each of the elements of an option must be developed in a way that it remains consistent with other elements of that action. Since the Gandhian method uses the definition of action in the Bhagvadgita, the elements of an action that need to be developed are the object of knowledge, knowledge, the knower, the means, the act, and the doer.

Once the set of desired consequences is known, there is no difficulty in recognising the object of knowledge: It is the achievement of the desired consequences. If the desired consequence is the removal of poverty in the local economy, the object of knowledge is to find the best way of doing so.

As this knowledge is to be gained by a knower, there is a subjective element involved. The subjectivity is not confined to the conscious bias of the knower. Even if the knower believes he has completely eliminated all bias, subjectivity would not disappear. For instance, the task of removing poverty in a local economy could be perceived differently by different people. For some it may just be a matter of increasing income. Others with greater awareness of local conditions may emphasise factors like the distance to the nearest source of drinking water. Not having to walk many miles each day to fetch water could make a big difference to the quality of life. Indeed, in societies where it is the duty of women to fetch water, providing a source of water close to the residential area could also reduce gender inequality. The subjective judgements of the knower can thus play an important role in the knowledge he gains. As the Gandhian method does not believe that subjectivity can be eliminated, it emphasises improving the quality of subjectivity.

In order to improve the quality of subjectivity, the Gandhian method requires the knower to develop two attributes. First, he has to be non-attached to the consequences of the action based on the knowledge he generates. This would make it easier for him to arrive at a fair judgement when dealing with the subjective elements of knowledge. The quality of subjective understanding does not, however, depend only on fairness. It is quite possible for a judgement to go wrong not only because the person making it is unfair, but also because his understanding of a particular situation is weak. The second attribute required from a knower thus relates to the quality of his judgements in a particular situation. For Gandhi such judgements were an indicator of knowledge itself. As he put it, 'True knowledge means the discrimination between the essential and the non-essential. The book-learning that does not give this power of discrimination is not knowledge but bookishness' (Gandhi, 1958–93, Vol. 52, p. 129). The perception of what is essential and what is non-essential would vary both across persons and over time. The same individual may judge a situation differently with the benefit of experience. In fact, the quality of the judgements would undergo a continuous process of interaction with experience. Once a judgement is made in a particular situation, the course of events in that situation will bring out the weaknesses and strengths of that judgement. This would influence the next judgement, which in turn will be evaluated by the next experience, and so on.

Ideally, the power of discrimination between the essential and the non-essential would improve over time. But this cannot be taken for granted. Much will depend on the lessons learnt from experience and the willingness to look at a particular situation in all its detail. Gandhi believed that this would only be possible if the knower made himself a part of the situation he was trying to understand. This would mean the economic policy maker cannot rely on secondary data alone, but would also need to provide a significant role for participant observation. Gandhi's emphasis on participant observation is reflected in his interaction with a major Indian social scientist of his time, Radhakamal Mukherjee. As Sugata Dasgupta argues on the basis of an incident narrated to him by Radhakamal Mukherjee:

> An intellectual who thinks he can write on [a] subject without becoming a part of the subject would be rebuked by no less a person than Gandhi himself. Dr. Radhakamal Mukherjee... had, it seems, engaged himself in a study of the working conditions of industrial labour in India. He had come to see

Gandhi with this news at a time when Gandhi was extremely busy with the affairs of the nation. Yet Gandhi canceled all his appointments and came out of his office eagerly to wait on the scientist. His hope was that Dr. Mukherjee was living among the laborers and collecting data all by himself. Gandhi quickly turned his back, sorely disappointed, calling off the interview as soon as he found out that Dr. Mukherjee did not live in the slums but had collected all his data from investigators appointed by him (Sugata Dasgupta, 1989, pp. 191–92).

The two attributes, of non-attachment and being a part of the situation that is being understood, may pull the knower in opposite directions. Non-attachment would be easier if the knower is distant from the subject of his knowledge; but this would hurt his understanding of the subtleties of a particular situation. And a knower who becomes a part of a situation may find it difficult to be non-attached. For instance, a knower seeking to improve the conditions of an impoverished tribe would need to live with them to understand the economic situation they find themselves in. But the time spent living with them would make it difficult to be non-attached to the consequences of the action the knower suggests. The ideal knower then faces the difficult challenge of not being attached to the consequences of the action based on the knowledge he generates, while at the same time being able to identify with the subject of his knowledge. In this task it would help if the knower recognises that the two attributes are not, strictly speaking, in direct conflict with each other. Non-attachment relates to the consequences of an action, while participant observation helps in improving the understanding of a particular situation. The skill of the knower in making this distinction in a real life situation will determine the quality of the subjective components of his or her knowledge.

In dealing with the objective elements of knowledge, the Gandhian method is guided by its inclusiveness. The method militates against reducing any situation to a single grand theory. Instead, it seeks to put together all the objective knowledge available at a point of time to develop a comprehensive picture of a particular economic situation. This would involve piecing together a number of economic models. The method, therefore, does not presume that models that may have emerged from different perceptions of the same situation are mutually exclusive. It is open to the possibility of models that focus on different factors having a role to play in understanding the same situation. Understanding a particular situation may require models of market behaviour provided by neo-classical economics as well as models of class interest provided by Marxian economics. Even when models are, in fact, mutually exclusive, the Gandhian method keeps open the possibility of using one model at one point of time and the other when the situation changes. The Marxian view of class interests may be useful in understanding the processes through which a feudal elite controls a remote rural market. But once the market is made genuinely free, the policy maker would have more to gain by using neo-classical models of market behaviour. In other words, the knower will need to judge which set of economic models are most appropriate in a given situation. He would also need to decide the relative importance to be given to each model in the set he has chosen. Clearly, the judgement would depend, among other things, on the quality of the model. A rigorous model that has been empirically tested is likely to carry greater weight than one that is not rigorous and is not supported by empirical evidence. In choosing a specific set of models as representative of the objective reality, the knower is automatically making a subjective demarcation between the objective and the subjective elements of knowledge.

Once a policy maker has understood a particular economic situation he or she will be in a position to choose the means of intervening in the economy. The inclusiveness of the Gandhian method will once again ensure that all possible instruments of intervention are considered. It will not presume that the state and the market are mutually exclusive instruments of intervention in the economy. There may be specific forms of state intervention that are not consistent with a free market, such as regulated prices. But there are also a number of forms of state intervention that are not inconsistent with a free market. Indeed, a free market requires the intervention of the state whenever the rules are broken. And even when the state and the market are inconsistent with each other, the Gandhian method allows the policy maker to choose either instrument of intervention depending on the situation. A policy maker can also opt for a free market at one point of time and then change tack and seek state intervention. Gandhi himself was a strong opponent of state controls, once even asking rhetorically: 'Must the voice of the people be drowned by the noise of the pundits who claim to know all about the virtue of controls?' (Gandhi, 1958-93, Vol. 90, p. 60). This resistance to controls was further strengthened by his emphasis on the rights of the individual. These rights included the right to learn from mistakes. As he continued in his rhetorical vein: 'Will not the people have any opportunity of committing mistakes and learning by them?' (ibid., p. 60). But he was equally clear that the scepticism about state control must not be turned into an absolute belief that held true irrespective of the situation. Gandhi recognised the possibility of situations emerging when controls became inevitable. He argued in 1947 that 'controls became necessary because of the fear of dishonesty and profiteering on the part of traders' (ibid., p. 309).

The Gandhian method does not also believe that the state and the market are the only instruments of intervention in the economy. Gandhi was particularly fond of using a direct appeal to the individual as an instrument of intervention in the economy. He often sought to change economic trends by getting individuals to change their economic behaviour. At times he was fairly successful, as when he got individual Indians to give up wearing foreign cloth. At other times he was less so, as when he tried to convince individual industrialists to function as trustees of their industries. But irrespective of Gandhi's own success or otherwise, the Gandhian method clearly considers a direct appeal to the individual as an instrument of intervention in the economy. To return to our example of removing poverty in the local economy, the Gandhian method would explore what can be achieved by direct appeals to individuals.

It may be possible for literate individuals to teach others to read and write, thereby improving the latter's ability to earn a livelihood. Thus in the choice of instruments of intervention in the economy too, the Gandhian method is inclusive and pluralistic.

The pluralism of the Gandhian method has its impact on the way a particular action is carried out as well. Pluralism implies a tolerance of a number of conflicting theories. This tolerance is essential in a method, like the Gandhian one, that recognises that knowledge is fallible. This fallibility makes the method stress the need to be sensitive to unintended consequences. This sensitivity makes the method wary of turmoil. This is in contrast to the approach of policy makers who believe in a grand theory. When there is unquestioning faith in a grand theory, whether it is of the market-knows-best variety or of the state-knows-best variety, the policy maker believes the sooner a change is brought about the better it is. Any pain that the implementation of a policy may generate is treated as a reason to move even more quickly to the new ideal system. This belief was, in fact, quite evident in both the Soviet socialist revolution as well as the shock therapy advocated, and followed, in the Russian Federation after the collapse of the Soviet Union. The Gandhian method, on the other hand, believes that even when it defines an ideal, it will not always be realised in reality. And the scope for unintended consequences in the movement towards this ideal calls for greater caution in the implementation of a policy. The Gandhian method thus advocates neither revolutions nor shock therapy.

On the contrary, the Gandhian method would keep open the option of changing tack at the first sign of severe unintended adverse consequences. It is quite possible that an action that seems best suited to achieve a particular consequence, turns out to be working against it. In such situations, the Gandhian method would demand that the specific action is immediately withdrawn. The clearest example of Gandhi's willingness to withdraw an action he was committed to comes from the sphere of politics. He suspended his civil disobedience movement in 1922 when his supporters turned violent in Chauri

Chaura.[4] It is not difficult to identify economic situations that may demand a similar reaction. State ownership can be justified on the grounds of helping the poor. But in reality it could turn out that the inefficiencies of the system actually harm the poor. In such situations the commitment must be to the consequences rather than the action itself, and the action must be withdrawn.

In order to be able to first justify an action and then justify its withdrawal, the individual implementing policy must have credibility. The doer in Gandhi's elements of an action must have the ability to convince the different groups in an economy that he is working towards the bargained consensus. In building this credibility he would have to make effective use of rhetoric. The importance Gandhi gave to this aspect of public policy is reflected in the many elements of rhetoric he used to convince others of his arguments. He saw a broader role for rhetoric than merely the written or spoken word. He recognised that the ability to persuade could extend to other elements like dress. Gandhi experimented a great deal with the use of dress to make his ideas more acceptable (Tarlo, 1996). He also developed most, if not all, of the elements of rhetoric that McCloskey has identified (McCloskey, 1994). He worked out in great detail the ethos, or the character he would assume when he expounded his ideas. Thus the transformation from the Western-educated barrister to the freedom fighter sparsely dressed in khadi. The latter character helped him identify with the poor in India. The picture of a frail man standing up to the might of the British empire added to his basic theme of non-violence. So much importance did he attach to this image that he refused to change his dress habits even under very adverse climatic conditions during a visit to England. He chose instead to stress this difference between him and the British rulers, as is evident from an oft-quoted anecdote. Asked whether he would meet the king in his usual dress, he replied the king had enough on for both of them (Fischer, 1954, p. 105).

This reply brings out another of the elements of rhetoric that McCloskey lists and Gandhi used most effectively—irony. The differences between Gandhi's ideas and Western thought were very substantial. This gap was further widened by the tendency in Western economic thought, after the Bolshevik revolution, to be preoccupied with either state ownership or private ownership. Given the size of this gap, Gandhi needed methods to reach out to an audience that was not conversant with the foundations on which his ideas were built. And he found irony useful. He would have agreed with McCloskey that 'jest protects and persuades' (McCloskey, 1994, p. 330). As another oft-cited quote goes, when asked what he thought of Western civilisation, Gandhi replied, it would be a good idea.

Even those elements of rhetoric that Gandhi appeared to be abandoning, were in fact only being strengthened in a novel way. Take, for instance, Gandhi's method of using the appeal of authority. As one biographer noted: All the props of the big man's impressiveness—the palace or historic mansion, the guards, the wait in the antechamber, the closed door about to open, the power of the office—were lacking. [But] Gandhi's on-the-earth simplicity, devoid of the appearances or reality of power, emphasized his authority' (Fischer, 1954, p. 142). He did not use any of the methods of establishing authority common among politicians, but Gandhi's lifestyle had an even greater authority of its own—that of a near-saint. Rather than abandoning appeals to authority, Gandhi was only redefining the same.

The uninhibited use of rhetoric, especially when seen in isolation, may appear to be opening the door for expediency. What is to stop an unscrupulous policy maker from using rhetoric to serve personal ends rather than to achieve the explicit set of desired consequences? The answer to this question would focus on two specific requirements of the Gandhian method. First, the method stresses the importance of moral force in a policy maker's armoury. The use of moral force on a sustained basis would be very difficult if a policy maker was guided purely by expediency. Indeed, rather than allowing policy makers to be guided by expediency, the Gandhian method demands they make sacrifices. It is these sacrifices that will provide them the moral force that will help convince others of their decisions. The second aspect of the Gandhian method that limits the scope for expediency in the use of rhetoric is the requirement of consistency. All the six elements of an action have to be consistent with each other. The policy maker cannot adopt a rhetoric that goes against other elements of an action.

The need for consistency also determines the relationship between other elements of an action. Though the knower and the doer may be two separate individuals, their contributions to an action will have to be consistent with each other. There is then no such thing as a good policy which cannot be implemented in a particular social situation. An action would only be considered effective if it can be implemented. Again, the act must be consistent with all the knowledge of the situation that is available at a point of time. An action that is based on knowledge that is not directly relevant to the area that is being affected by the action would also be inconsistent. Indeed, the internal consistency of an action could very well call for very different prescriptions for different situations. In other words, consistency in the Gandhian method refers to all elements of an action being consistent with each other. It does not require the same element to be consistent across different situations. Faced with a high rate of inflation it would be perfectly consistent for a policy maker to look at monetary options in some situations while in others he considers other options like removing transport bottlenecks to improve availability. The Gandhian method thus does not in any way reduce the importance of consistency. It is only when consistency is evaluated in terms of prescriptions alone that the method may appear inconsistent, as its prescriptions can keep changing. Gandhi himself had to face the charge of inconsistency and chose to brush it aside, claiming that 'if I am inconsistent, I am wisely so' (Gandhi, 1958–93, Vol. 45, p. 340).

This outline of the Gandhian method in the economy stresses the many dimensions of its inclusiveness. It is inclusive in terms of the inputs it requires for an analysis. It is inclusive in terms of the factors that must be considered and the models that can be used. And, equally significantly, it is also inclusive in a methodological sense. Its focus on action, and broad definition of an action, ensures that no methodological issue falls out of its purview. It concerns itself with not just finding answers to specific questions, but also with the process of arriving at those questions. Its elaborate method of choosing a set of desired consequences gives the process of choosing the questions to be asked as much importance as the specific process of finding the right answers. More than the specific innovations in the Gandhian method, such as Swadeshi and Trusteeship, it is its inclusiveness that marks it out to be a fundamentally different method of formulating and implementing economic policy.

GANDHI AND HIS METHOD

In our outline of the Gandhian method, a recurring theme has been the fallibility of those using the method. As long as betting quotients are less than 1, no claims are being made to certainty. And even when a confident policy maker adopts a betting quotient of 1, the fact that the Gandhian method functions on relative truth would suggest that this certainty need not be justified. This brings us to a problem not unlike those faced by statisticians choosing a level of significance. When they postulate that they will be right 99 times out of 100, they also imply that they will be wrong one time in a hundred. Similarly, if the fallibility implicit in the Gandhian method is to be justified, we must identify cases where Gandhi's judgements went wrong.

A comprehensive analysis of Gandhi and the way he used his method is a large exercise that is well beyond the scope of this book. But a look at some of the issues where history has proved Gandhi wrong does help to identify the points where those using the Gandhian method can be misled. And there are at least two parts of the Gandhian method that sometimes lend themselves to judgements that go against some of the basic premises of that method.

First, there is the danger of, what can be called, disguised absolutism. There is little doubt that the Gandhian method is built on pluralism. But the sanction to use all elements, including rhetoric and moral force, to convince others of a particular position can lead to the faith in that position becoming absolute.

For instance, Gandhi's advocacy of decentralisation or his opposition to the excesses of modern technology were subject to the pluralism of his method. His concept of decentralisation did not rule out a role for centralised control nor did his comments on the damage caused by railways prevent him from extensively using the Indian railway network. But his consistent advocacy of decentralisation and his opposition to modern technology made these ideas appear absolutely essential to any Gandhian understanding, irrespective of the situation. Gandhi himself underestimated the possibility of new factors completely changing a situation. He grossly underestimated the ability of technology to meet rapidly growing demand through more efficient use of limited resources. He believed 'that if India becomes industrialised, we shall need a Nadirshah to find out other worlds to exploit, that we shall have to pit ourselves against the naval and military power of Britain and Japan and America, of Russia and Italy' (Gandhi, 1958–93, Vol. 62, p. 145). This view was, no doubt, based on a universalised view of consequentialism, where exploiting one country to serve another was unacceptable. His fears about the adequacy of resources to meet the needs of industrialisation were also the result of his belief that every citizen of the world should be able to get the benefits of industrialisation. But the crisis of resources has not been so severe as to require the spartan existence that Gandhi advocated. The dramatic advances in technology since Gandhi's time have certainly expanded the material well-being that available resources can provide. There may still be some truth in Gandhi's oft-quoted view that nature provides enough for every man's need, but not for every man's greed (cited, for instance, in Schumacher, 1977, p. 29). But technology has allowed a much more liberal view of what is every man's need.

This disguised absolutism can be particularly distorting when the morality on which it is based does not have universal acceptance. This is perhaps best seen in the case that Gandhi and his followers built for prohibiting the consumption of liquor. If we use a morality where the consumption of liquor is itself not good, the Gandhian method could, and did, end up advocating prohibition. But if we were to use a morality that did not see the consumption of liquor as bad in itself, it would have to be evaluated in terms of the consequences of prohibition. Unintended consequences such as the loss of life due to the consumption of illicit liquor would also have to be taken into account. And once these factors enter the calculation, the appropriate judgement could be less dogmatic about prohibition.

The second major source for errors of judgement in the Gandhian method is related to the role of ideals. The ideals are supposed to provide the goals towards which society can and should move. But if these ideals are too distant from the current reality, they could be termed unattainable and ignored. This was the fate of several of the ideals Gandhi advocated, like Trusteeship. Indeed, by the time reality makes some of these ideals less unrealistic, the fact that Gandhi had predicted movement in this direction is forgotten. In an era where labour and capital viewed the industry entirely in terms of the factor of production they represented, Gandhi's concept of Trusteeship was clearly idealistic and perhaps even irrelevant. But over the years the owners of labour power and capital have had to distance themselves from views that saw the economy entirely in terms of either labour or capital alone. Employee stock options, for instance, provide a reason for labour to consider a situation from the point of view of capital as well. Professional managers too have to take decisions that represent the interests of several, if not all, stakeholders. Trusteeship may still be an unattainable ideal, but its emphasis on the need to rise above partisan interests in a corporation are beginning to be recognised.

Gandhi's own practice of his method thus indicates that it remains sensitive to the quality of subjective judgements. But that only makes an even stronger case for improving the quality of subjective judgements rather than trying to pretend these judgements have only a marginal influence on policy.

NOTES

1. Louis Fischer notes that at a meeting of textile millworkers, one man said, 'I am one of the unemployed, but if I was in India I would say the same thing that Mr Gandhi is saying' (Fischer, 1954, p. 106).

2. The events leading to the payment of Rs 550 million to Pakistan and the reaction of the assassins are recounted in Fischer (1954, pp. 183–89).
3. Gandhi's staunchest followers who were in the first Indian government after Independence argued strongly against the payment and only gave in when their leader proved to be adamant.
4. For an account of the event, see Fischer (1954, pp. 70–71).

4

Methodological Outposts

In placing the Gandhian method in the context of contemporary debate, it is easy to get lost in the detail. There are aspects of his thought that make interesting comparisons with ideas that developed later in the twentieth century. His concept of Trusteeship, for instance, has some similarity with Rawl's Original Position.[1] Trusteeship is based on the premise that the most fair solutions to a conflict of interests would emerge in situations where those owning a particular factor of production believed they were only holding that in trust for society at large. In other words, the individual did not address the situation entirely in terms of his self-interest. In Rawl's Original Position too fairness is achieved by getting people to define principles of fairness before they know where their self-interest lies. Again, similarities can be found between the deontological consequentialism that Sen advocates and Gandhi's inclusive consequentialism.[2] But such details, though interesting and worthy of further study, are not our prime concern here. Since our concern in this exercise is with the Gandhian method, our focus must be on the response of the Gandhian method to specific methodological issues.

Identifying the methodological issues that confront the maker of economic policy is a task that has not received sufficient attention. When economists dealing with policy issues do speak of method, they rarely go beyond specific techniques, like the method of collecting and analysing data. The philosophical issues that are implicit in those techniques do not receive much attention. This situation has not been fundamentally altered by the growing interest in economic methodology over the last two decades of the twentieth century.[3] This interest has resulted in a vibrant debate over a number of philosophical issues underlying the method that economists use. But the impact of this work in economic methodology on the actual practice of economists making policy has been rather limited. Economic methodologists have had to spend a considerable amount of time at the first step of arguing that methodology does, in fact, matter. Not suprisingly they have tended, over time, to concentrate on specific philosophical issues rather than develop an active link between policy making and economic methodology.[4] They have, arguably, been more influenced by trends in the philosophy of science rather than by trends in economic policy making. In the process, the growing body of literature on economic methodology has only served to open up a new specialised field in economics rather than influence the method used by economists in general. Indeed, the status of economic methodology as a separate sub-branch of economics, instead of being an influence on all branches of the science, appears to have been accepted by some contributors to the study of economic methodology (Gustafsson, 1993, p. ix).

Despite the revival of interest in economic methodology, therefore, most economists interested in policy continue to have little time for issues of method. They seem to prefer the adage that those who do, do and those who don't, discuss methodology. Against this backdrop of a general indifference to method on the part of those making economic policy, it becomes necessary to go back to basics in identifying the methodological questions that need to be answered. At every stage in the formulation and implementation of policy there are different methodological issues that arise. The attempt here is to identify some of the more important of these issues and outline the response of the Gandhian method to them. Some of these questions have undoubtedly received considerable attention in the debate on economic methodology; but others, particularly those related to the implementation of policy, have remained outside that debate.

CHOICE OF THE PROBLEM

In much of contemporary economics, the choice of the questions to be asked rarely gets as much attention as the process of finding the answers to those questions. Indeed, in the few discussions of method by economists who are not specialists in methodology, the choice of an issue is often taken as given. Take Krugman's advice on how an economist should go about his business. His first step is: 'Figure out what you think about an issue, working back and forth among verbal intuition, evidence, and as much math as you need' (Krugman, 1998b). In other words, the choice of an issue does not require explicit norms.

This attitude to the issues to be raised may be a reflection of the Popperian influence on economics. As Feyerabend argued, there is no clearly defined basis in Popper's method for deciding why a particular problem should be studied (see Feyerabend, 1978). In the absence of such norms an issue can be chosen for any reason, from being the personal interest of an economist, to explaining a real life economic crisis. This eclectic basis for the choice of issues to be studied contributes to the phenomenon of economists always playing, in Krugman's words, 'theoretical catch up' (Krugman, 1998a). The ivory tower economist, who just happens to be interested in an issue, may not even be keen to ensure that his or her analysis is useful in a crisis. And the economists who wait for the real world to determine their agenda, would, by definition, be following events rather than predicting them.

This absence of adequate attention to the choice of a problem could also result in a less than efficient specification of a problem. Contemporary economics often does not spend too much time on deciding whether the problem is correctly formulated. This is, in fact, one of the risks of the Popperian method. As Feyrabend pointed out, 'This characterization does not consider that problems may be wrongly formulated, that one may enquire about properties of things and processes which later views declare to be non-existent. Problems of this kind are not solved, they are dissolved and removed from the domain of legitimate inquiry' (Feyerabend, 1978, p. 274). Economic policy makers are particularly prone to such wrongly formulated problems when they address developments that economic theory has not yet caught up with. A widely read example would be the debate between Oskar Lange and Fred Taylor in the 1930s on whether a socialist economy was 'impracticable' (Lange and Taylor, 1976). But this problem was not considered a meaningful one when the Soviet Union reached the peak of its economic powers. And though the socialist economy in the Soviet Union collapsed under the weight of its inefficiencies, the very fact that it existed for over seven decades does make the debate on it being 'impracticable' quite irrelevant. The problem was misstated as whether a socialist economy was practicable when the real question was whether it would be efficient enough to survive.

The Gandhian method, in contrast, pays much greater attention to the process of choosing the questions to be raised. The focus of the method is on an action. The questions to be raised, that is the object of knowledge, form just one component of an action. These questions must then be consistent with the other components of the action, namely, knowledge, the knower, the means, the doer, and the act itself. The choice of an action would itself be determined by a variety of factors in a particular situation, including the persons or groups involved, the extent to which they are empowered, and whether they adhere to any given system of fairness. But once several actions are identified as the available options, they will determine the questions that are asked.

The need for consistency among all the elements of an action would reduce the scope for a mismatch between policy formulation and implementation. When policy is formulated and implemented by two distinct groups, they need not always work in harmony. Free market policies could be implemented only half-heartedly by a bureaucracy that has an interest in state control. Conversely, those implementing policies based on state control may be attracted by the rent opportunities that market forces offer. This mismatch is heightened when those formulating policy believe that their policies have not been effectively implemented and those in charge of implementation believe those formulating policy have no understanding of ground realities. The Gandhian method's insistence on consistency between all elements of an action would rule out the formulation of a policy that does not have the support of those implementing it.

Beyond the minimum requirement of consistency, the elements of an action can also influence each other. For instance, the recognition that there is a subjective element to knowledge makes the Gandhian method sensitive to the possibility of error. It then becomes imperative to be tolerant of conflicting theories in the realm of knowledge. For the means of an action to be consistent with this tolerance, any form of coercion would be ruled out. Instead of coercion the means would rely on persuasion. The means of persuasion would include the use of moral force. This emphasis on morality in the means of an action would, in turn, influence the realm of knowledge. Economic analysis in the realm of knowledge cannot then be separated from ethical analysis.

The need for consistency between different elements of an action, as well as their interaction with each other, defines boundaries within which the Gandhian method operates. For instance, the emergence of tolerance as a critical aspect of the method demands a strict adherence to non-violence in thought and deed. The existence of these boundaries also serves to prevent the pluralism of the Gandhian method from slipping into complete anarchy. The pluralism has to operate within these boundaries and cannot adopt a framework where anything goes.

These limits to the pluralism of the Gandhian method may appear to limit its inclusiveness. It does rule out options that, say, involve violence. But the effect of these boundaries on the inclusiveness of the method must not be overestimated. It is important to recognise that the restrictions are placed on the process of choosing an action and not at the earlier point of identifying all the factors involved. In other words, when identifying the factors that need to be studied, the method remains inclusive. There are no predetermined restrictions on the questions to be raised. It is possible that some of these questions are not properly formulated, and others may dissolve over time. But with there being no limits on questions being raised from diverse perspectives, the chances of a critical question going unasked will be reduced. To that extent there is less chance of being surprised by events.

MODELS AND EXPLANATION

One of the few methodological issues on which there remains considerable attention even among economists who are not specialised in methodology is the role of economic models. On the few occasions when economists, other than those specialised in economic methodology, outline their method, they do so in a way that provides a prominent role for economic models. This is a pattern that goes back at least to the time of Alfred Marshall. As Marshall famously summarised his method:

> (1) Use mathematics as a shorthand language, rather than an engine of inquiry. (2) Keep to them till you have done. (3) Translate into English. (4) Then illustrate by examples that are important in real life. (5) Burn the mathematics. (6) If you can't succeed in 4, burn 3 (cited in Sills and Merton, 1991).

The precise steps that economists would like to follow could differ from the ones listed by Marshall. Krugman for one lays out a slightly different routine (Krugman 1998b). But the underlying assumption, that economics is best understood by reducing reality to an abstract economic model, is widely accepted in economics. Most economists would agree with Partha Dasgupta that, 'The point, as always, is that if we do not have a good model, we will not know what are the possible outcomes of any given policy; we will not know how to choose among contending policies' (Dasgupta, 1992, p. 22).

This preoccupation with models has not been without its critics. The arcane algebra and the unrealistic assumptions of economic models have been particularly prone to criticism.[5] Such criticism, more often than not, builds a case for rejecting economic models altogether. Economists who use models counter this criticism by arguing that abstract models are essential for rigorous analysis; that economists need to abstract from real life when trying to understand a specific phenomenon. As Maki argues, 'Any theory involves an isolation of a limited set of entities from all other ingredients in a total situation' (Maki, 1993a, p. 28). The isolation of a set of key factors in each economic model is thus an essential ingredient of rigorous economic analysis. The nature of this criticism and the response has tended to give the debate on the role of models in economics an all-or-nothing character. The issue has been largely reduced to a choice between rigour on the one hand, and a reliance on intuitive judgement on the other. Those preferring rigour stick to economic models while those emphasising intuitive judgement shun models.

Rigour and intuitive judgement need not, however, be mutually exclusive. Critics of economic models cannot, and generally do not, find fault with its rigour. Typically they concentrate their attack on the inability of a model to provide an approximation to reality. Indeed, the poor record of models as approximations to reality has even prompted successful economists to question their value. As early as 1983, the Nobel laureate Wassily Leontief went so far as to state:

> Year after year economic theorists continue to produce scores of mathematical models and to explore in great detail their formal properties; and the econometricians fit algebraic functions of all possible shapes to essentially the same sets of data without being able to advance, in any perceptible way, a systematic understanding of the structure and the operations of a real economic system (Leontief, 1983, pp. x-xi).

This criticism may not always be justified. As Krugman has so eloquently argued, there are formal models using arcane algebra that can be very useful in real life situations, particularly the works of auction theorists and finance theorists (Krugman, 1998b). But the value of a model as an approximation to reality does tend to vary. It is easier to develop such a model when there are fewer factors at play. It also helps if these factors are entirely predictable and if there is a limited role for subjectivity either as a factor in the model or in the interpretation of other factors. It is thus often possible to come up with accurate rigorous models of technical movements in stock exchanges, at least over limited periods of time. But in a more complex real life situation where there is a multiplicity of social, economic and political factors at play, such as the Asian crisis of 1997, the models may be less accurate. This has led, quite understandably, to increasing scepticism about the value of such large all-explaining models. Hutchison, for instance, argues:

> General theories require general laws, or substantial reliable generalizations as a basis. There have, on the whole, for much of the past two hundred years, been rather more in the way of such substantial general propositions to serve as a basis for microeconomics than for macroeconomics, though even for microeconomics the basic generalizations are somewhat tenuous (Hutchison, 1981, p. 257).

The scepticism over general theories has contributed to a large number of economists opting for models with a more limited scope. This is achieved primarily by narrowing the focus of their models. Where the focus cannot be narrowed, as in General Equilibrium Theory, the scope is reduced by limiting the factors that are considered. This is evident from Morishima's complaint: 'The number of actors on the stage in this GET [General Equilibrium Theory] world are far too few' (Morishima, 1992, p. 71). Indeed, much of economics today is dominated by narrowly focused formal models. Economists seem to believe that in order to protect their rigour they need to compromise on comprehensiveness.

But the need to choose between comprehensiveness and rigour arises primarily because models are expected to be approximations to reality. This is an expectation that has no obvious justification. An insistence that models must approximate to reality can, in fact, distort the policy maker's perspective in several ways. First, the key factors that are analysed in a model are typically derived from one particular situation. To assume that another situation must be the same in all its detail is obviously unrealistic. The softer assumption that the two situations are similar can also go wrong; factors that are peripheral in one situation can have a relatively more significant role in another. Judging the relative importance of each factor through empirical testing is also not as effective an option as it may appear at first sight. Policy makers often have to react without the luxury of waiting for detailed empirical evaluation of a situation. And when they find the time for empirical verification, it must be remembered that these tests are not as infallible as they are sometimes made out to be. As Mark Blaug has pointed out, 'The so-called Duhem-Quine thesis demonstrates that it is just as difficult conclusively to falsify a hypothesis as to verify it because every test of a hypothesis is in fact a joint test of the hypothesis in question, the quality of the data, the measuring instruments employed and a host of auxiliary hypotheses stipulating the particular circumstances of the test; in the event of a falsification, we can never assign guilt unambiguously to the central hypothesis under examination' (Blaug, 1994, p. 111). This problem becomes acute if the test of an economic theory itself alters the initial conditions of the test. 'Conducting a test of the relationship between the money supply and the price level may alter expectations in such a way that the initial conditions (which were true "initially") are not true after the test (or if the "same" test were conducted again)' (Hands, 1993, p. 64). If no test is perfect, there can be a variety of tests that are acceptable. It could then be possible to design a test in a way that a hypothesis would be accepted.

Second, the value of a model as an approximation to reality could also be eroded if the unit of analysis it uses is not the appropriate one. A particular relationship could follow one pattern when seen individually and quite another when seen as a part of an organic whole. To use a Keynesian example, while thrift may be a virtue individually, it could at a macro level reduce demand, income and the overall quantum of saving. The organic whole cannot then be understood as the sum of its parts. As Gerrard puts it in his interpretation of Keynes' views:

> ... knowledge cannot be formulated fully if phenomena are not atomistic in nature but rather organic. Organic unities can only be grasped intuitively and as wholes. An organic unity can be analysed only in terms of fragments of form. By its very nature, an organic unity defies complete reduction to its constituent parts. An organic whole is always more than the sum of its parts (Gerrard, 1992, pp. 7–8).

The scope to use a model based on an inappropriate unit of analysis is greater than is often recognised. In the prelude to the Asian crisis, for instance, it would have been perfectly rational for individual companies to believe they were insuring their projects against failure by acquiring additional land at a time when real estate prices were booming. But as more companies followed this model it created a real estate bubble that had to burst. If this was not recognised before the crisis, a part of the blame must lie with the tendency to treat individual companies and their projects as the primary units of analysis.

A third source of error when using models as approximations to reality is a leftover of ideological theories. In the simple system where ideologies were based on a core economic model, the instrument of intervention was built into the model. A free market model would underestimate, if not ignore, the role of the state. And economic models that emerged from the Soviet Union underestimated, if not ignored, the role of markets. While there were a few models that suggested a combination of state intervention and a free market, such as variations of the Indian Second Plan model, these were more the exception than the rule.[6] In most cases, the models advocated a major role either for the market or the state. Within the set of free market models some were even more specific in the instruments they advocated, as in the case of models that relied almost exclusively on monetary policy to intervene in the economy. The potential for using a multiplicity of instruments has now been recognised more in practice, with the rise of 'Pragmatism' in economic policy making, particularly after the collapse of the Soviet Union. But since a variety of policies could be justified on the grounds of being pragmatic, the policy maker still has a choice. And he could prefer an instrument he used before he gave up his ideology for Pragmatism. A Monetarist-turned-Pragmatist may tend to use a tight monetary policy even at a time when there is a liquidity crunch.

It is thus important not to expect models to be approximations to reality. If we abandon this expectation, models can explain specific relationships which are not evident in the larger picture of reality. We can then have both a comprehensive picture of the economy as well as rigorous models. Dropping this expectation would, of course, imply that models cannot be used directly to predict the course of economic events. Instead, models would form part of a larger method of understanding the economy. In other words, a method would have to define a precise role for models in a larger assessment of a situation.

This is precisely what the Gandhian method aims to do. By explicitly ruling out a reliance on any grand theory, the method makes it clear that no single model can claim to be an approximation to reality. There is instead a larger analysis with a focus on consequences. This focus makes it imperative that all the factors that influence the consequences, directly or indirectly, are taken into account. Indeed, omitting factors from an analysis, even if they were relatively minor, would be treated as a serious shortcoming of an analysis based on the Gandhian method. The method would also allow for the significance of each factor to vary across different situations. The required consistency is to be found in the predefined morality, the focus on consequentialism and the goodness of the actions in themselves. As consistency is not sought in the prescriptions, there is no commitment to a predefined set of prescribed actions. Models can then be used to understand specific relations within the larger picture. The relationships understood in these models may explain only a small part of the larger picture.

Or they may interact with other relationships in a way that the consequences are different from what the model predicts. While the model would then be an integral part of the analysis, there would be no reason to expect it, in every situation, to be an approximation to the complete picture.

Within this larger framework, the precise role that a model plays in a policy action could vary across situations. In some situations, of hyper-inflation, restricting money supply may be the most important element of a policy action. In other situations, such as when there are transport bottlenecks, money supply may not be the cornerstone of a policy action against inflation. Again, the unit of analysis too could vary. A desired consequence like the removal of poverty in a village would require a set of actions that could include initiatives at both the macro and the micro level. It could, for instance, include both a macro initiative to keep down prices as well as a local initiative to improve the individual's ability to invest. The quality of the assessment of a particular situation would also depend on the willingness of the policy maker to choose the most appropriate instrument of intervention in the economy. He or she cannot get too attached to either state oriented instruments or market oriented ones alone. It was this insistence on a multiplicity of instruments that kept Gandhi largely out of the debate on the state versus the markets in the first half of the twentieth century.

The policy maker thus has to merge the rigorous analysis of precise models with the intuitive judgement of deciding the best action, based on a combination of models, for a particular situation. Unlike the more traditional critics of economic models, the Gandhian method's differences are not with models, per se, but with treating individual economic models as approximations to reality. The Gandhian method would only use a model as an input into an analysis of the consequences of a particular action in a specific situation.

As inputs into a larger exercise, economic models would have two very critical roles to play. First, they would serve to give the analysis the benefit of abstraction. This would allow for a rigorous analysis of a specific cost-effect relationship in isolation.

Such rigorous models would improve the quality of inputs into the larger analysis of the consequences of an action. Second, the Gandhian method could use economic models as an ideal, with the clear understanding that this ideal would never be achieved in reality. In Gandhi's terminology the model would be absolute while the reality would be relative. The model could then be an ideal for a policy maker to pursue. The closer he can get the economy to the ideal the better it would be, though the ideal itself would never become reality.

In using an economic model as an abstraction, an ideal or both, the Gandhian method calls for both rigorous analysis and intuitive judgement. In the process it goes back to Gandhi's distinction between reason and faith. There are some statements the validity of which can be determined by reason alone. And then there would be others where inputs from both within the realm of reason and outside it would also be considered, with the condition that reason always has precedence over faith. An empirically well-tested rigorous economic model would then be preferred to any contradictory explanation that is either outside the realm of reason or is less well tested or rigorous.

THE DEMARCATION QUESTION

The contention that reason must gain precedence over faith implies a clear demarcation between the two. The search for the criteria for such a demarcation brings us to the debate on a similar issue in the philosophy of science. The demarcation between reason and faith can be treated as an approximation to the Popperian demarcation between science and non-science. While a detailed exposition of the debate in the philosophy of science will be beyond the scope of the present exercise, an outline of the issues involved helps us recognise the Gandhian method's demarcation between reason and faith.

The need for such a demarcation would not arise if policy makers could fall back on a knowledge base that is perfect; where they know all that they need to know and where there can be no doubts about what they know. But in reality such perfect knowledge is elusive. And this is not simply because policy makers often do not have all the information they may require. More significantly, they can never be certain that what they know is absolutely true. A search for the absolute truth comes up against Hume's problem of induction, which is that no matter how many facts they have they can never be absolutely certain that what they know is true. To cite an oft-cited example, no matter how many black crows we see, we can never be absolutely certain there is no white crow in existence.

This is a problem that economists concerned with policy have been well aware of. As one neo-Keynesian summarised Keynes's views on the limits of human knowledge:

> Knowledge is always provisional in the face of an unknown future. This is the problem of uncertainty enshrined in Hume's famous statement of the problem of induction .... Knowledge is [also] incomplete because of 'the complexities and the interdependence of the real world'. Even if the world is atomistic; so that the reductionist project is legitimate, the multitude of causal factors involved will always render our explanations incomplete (Gerrard, 1992, p. 7).

The strongest claims to having solved the problem of induction have been made by Popper. He interprets the problem of induction as one of trying to infer a theory from singular statements that are verified by experience. This is flawed because verification, as in the case of finding the colour of all crows, can never be sufficient. 'Theories are, therefore, never empirically verifiable" (Popper, 1959, p. 40). The key to the solution of the problem of induction is to replace verifiability with an alternative criterion to justify a scientific statement. For Popper, falsifiability would be a superior criterion to decide whether a statement is scientific. Once a theory is falsifiable there is an objective method of deciding whether that theory should be accepted or not. Obviously, not all statements are falsifiable. To use Popper's own example, the statement 'It will rain or not rain here tomorrow' cannot be refuted while the statement 'It will rain here tomorrow' can be refuted (see Popper, 1959,

p. 41). The criterion of falsifiability thus ensures that the only statements that can be considered scientific are those that can be refuted. By confining science to statements that can be empirically refuted, it becomes possible to develop a set of objectively acceptable scientific theories. Thus, in order to demarcate between science and non-science, it is 'not the verifiability but the falsifiability of a system [that] is to be taken as a criterion for demarcation' (Popper, 1959, p. 40). In other words, 'It must be possible for an empirical scientific system to be refuted by experience' (ibid., p. 41).

Implicit in this view of science is the contention that it is never, and will never be, possible to positively state that some statement is the absolute truth. Even theories that have survived the most rigorous testing at any one point of time, can always be falsified by new evidence. Indeed, as the facts generated by experience increase, theories that were once believed to be true are continuously being falsified. Popper thus needs to operate with less than the absolute truth. This is made explicit when he sets out to identify the object of 'rational belief:

> It is, I submit, not the truth, but what we may call the truthlikeness (or verisimilitude) of the theories of science, so far as they have stood up to severe criticism, including tests. What we believe (rightly or wrongly) is not that Newton's theory or Einstein's theory is true, but that they are good approximations to the truth, though capable of being superseded by better ones (Popper, 1983, p. 57).

Over time as the facts thrown up by experience falsify theories they would be replaced by better theories.[7] This would bring science closer and closer to the absolute truth, though it will never get there. As Popper put it:

> Truth—absolute truth—remains our aim; and it remains the implicit standard of our criticism: almost all criticism is an attempt to refute the theory criticized; that is to say, to show that it is not true.... Thus we are always searching for a true theory (a true and relevant theory), even though we can

never give reasons (positive reasons) to show that we have actually found the true theory we have been searching for. At the same time we may have good reasons—that is, good critical reasons—for thinking we have learned something important: that we have progressed towards the truth (Popper, 1983, p. 25).

Whatever the merits of this system in the realm of logic, it runs into serious difficulties in practice. In reality, the distinction between the scientific and the non-scientific is not as clear as Popper would like. The two can influence each other. For instance, Popper does not consider metaphysical statements to be scientific. And yet the metaphysical can influence the scientific. As Popper has himself acknowledged, he did 'not think it possible to eliminate all "metaphysical elements" from science: they are too closely interwoven with the rest' (ibid., p. 179). Indeed, Popper argues that 'science has at all times been profoundly influenced by metaphysical ideas; certain metaphysical ideas and problems ... have dominated the development of science for centuries, as regulative ideas; while others ... have by degrees turned into scientific theories' (ibid., pp. 159–60). He goes on to argue that 'there cannot be any sharp demarcation between science and metaphysics; and the significance of the demarcation, if any, should not be overrated' (ibid., p. 161).

But, in reality, the Popperian system has an inherent tendency to stress the importance of demarcation. In part, this is because Popper sees a significant role for demarcation in scientific method:

> The problem of demarcation is ... closely related, historically as well as logically, to ... the central problem of the philosophy of knowledge. For the problem of how to adjudicate or decide among competing theories or beliefs leads ... to the problem of whether it is possible or impossible to justify a theory rationally; and this, in its turn, leads to the problem of distinguishing between, or of demarcating, rational theories and irrational beliefs (ibid., pp. 161–62).

To this philosophical necessity is added a more practical compulsion. For Popper, the practical relevance of the problem of demarcation lay in the need to prevent false theories from being presented as scientific. As he saw it, in the absence of an emphasis on testability, theories such as Freud's psychoanalysis and Marx's materialist interpretation of history were argued in an uncritical manner. 'A great number of arguments were marshaled in their support. But criticism and counter arguments were regarded as hostile, as symptoms of a willful refusal to admit the manifest truth; and they were therefore met with hostility rather than with arguments' (Popper, 1983, p. 162). And this failure had an immense practical importance in a social situation where acceptance of a theory as scientific could be used to justify any action including the taking of human lives.

In order to prevent pseudo-scientific theories being used to justify oppressive systems, there had to be a search for stricter and stricter norms for deciding what is scientific. Thus, even as he insisted that the significance of demarcation should not be overrated, Popper went on to add: 'In spite of this, I contend that the problem of demarcation is highly significant. It is so, not because there is any intrinsic merit in classifying theories, but because a number of genuine and important problems are closely linked with it; in fact, all the main problems of the logic of science' (ibid., p. 161).

Popper tries to overcome this contradiction between the need for a rigorously defined demarcation and the reality of an essentially fuzzy demarcation between science and metaphysics by shifting the focus to distinguishing between rational theories and irrational beliefs. He then argues that to identify the distinction between rational theories and irrational beliefs with the distinction between scientific theories and metaphysical ones would be rash (see ibid., p. 162). Having confined himself to the demarcation between rational theories and irrational beliefs, Popper only considers as scientific theories that are testable, and where the rigour of these tests is consistently increased.

This Popperian response to the reality of a weak demarcation can be challenged at several levels. The increasing degree of rigour in tests has its value in understanding the growth of a science. As Popper put it, 'The rate of progress may be very high just in a field in which the standards of criticism and of testing are very high' (Popper, 1983, p. 65). But as the norms of testing get more and more rigorous, in order to prevent a false theory from being accepted, there is an increased possibility of rejecting statements that may, in fact, be true.

This weakness of falsification is particularly significant for economists because of what has been called the 'Popperian dominance' of economic methodology (Maki, 1993a, p. 5).[8] This domination contributed to the weaknesses of falsification being quite widespread in the practice of economic analysis. As Blaug points out: 'Whenever we say a relationship is statistically significant at a level of significance of as low as 5 percent or even 1 percent, we commit ourselves to the decision that the risk of accepting a false hypothesis is greater than the risk of rejecting a true one, and this decision is not itself a matter of logic, nor can it be justified simply by pointing to the history of past scientific accomplishments' (Blaug, 1980, p. 22).

The adverse consequences of an excessively rigorous demarcation are accentuated when seen from a policy maker's perspective. When confronted with a situation where the available evidence is insufficient, the criterion of rigorous testability can become a severe drawback. This is evident from Popper's guide to practical action. 'As to practical actions, I should be ready to base them ... on the best theory in its field, *provided it has been well tested*' (emphasis added) (Popper, 1983, p. 65). Clearly, this method would not be of much use as a guide for action in fields where theories are not well tested. And as the acceptable degree of rigour in the field keeps growing, so will the group of theories that will not be considered well tested.

The social reasons Popper cites for his preferring a more-rigorous-than-justifiable demarcation are also not beyond dispute. While pseudo-scientific theories have undoubtedly had a high social cost, they need not be, perhaps cannot be, fought from the realm of scientific method alone. Even if Marxists were prevented from claiming their theories to be scientific, there is little evidence to show that it, would have had anything more than a marginal effect on the actions of leaders like Stalin. Indeed, by Popper's own rigorous criteria, this contention would be unscientific.

There have been attempts to make the demarcation less rigid. Foremost among these attempts is the import of Lakatos's ideas into economic methodology.[9] Lakatos addresses both the issue of the focus on a problem being too narrow and the harshness of falsifiability as a criterion for demarcation. He shifts the focus away from a specific problem by focusing instead on the broader category of scientific research programmes. These programmes are defined in terms of a hardcore that cannot be refuted. Around this hardcore is a protective belt where rules are laid out on how research is to be conducted. If these rules not only explain away anomalies but also lead to the generation of novel facts, the programme is progressive but if it only succeeds in explaining away anomalies without generating novel facts, the programme is degenerating. In other words, the criterion for assessing a research programme is not falsifiability, but the ability to generate novel facts. Over time the degenerating scientific research programmes would fade away to be replaced by the progressive ones.

This methodology of scientific research programmes has been attractive to economists, not the least because it allows for the coexistence of different scientific research programmes at the same time—one of the realities of modern economic analysis. But economic methodologists who have tried to identify specific scientific research programmes in economics have found the definition of a scientific research programme in terms of an invariant hardcore to be too narrow (Backhouse, 1994, p. 176).

A more serious objection to the methodology of scientific research programmes comes from philosophers of science. Lakatos's contention that science moves from one scientific research programme to another implies that statements that are considered unacceptable today could become acceptable in some future scientific research programme. It is then not possible to reject any statement in totality. As Feyerabend points out, 'The methodology of research programmes was introduced with the purpose of aiding rationalism. Yet it cannot condemn a single action as "irrational"' (Feyerabend, 1978, p. 204). In other words, if falsifiability was too strong a criterion for demarcation, generating novel facts is too weak a criterion. If falsifiability rejected statements that could be true, generating novel facts includes statements that may be false.

The apparent impossibility of arriving at an acceptable criterion for demarcation has led to a questioning of the need for such a demarcation. At a rather extreme level, Feyerabend argues: 'All methodologies have their limitations and the only "rule" that survives is "anything goes"' (ibid., p. 296). Rorty distinguishes between those who wish to ground solidarity in objectivity and those, like himself, who wish to reduce objectivity to solidarity (Rorty, 1996). This rejection of objectivity calls for new perceptions of reality. Among these alternative perceptions is that of the constructivists who argue that 'the only independent reality is beyond the reach of our knowledge and language. A known world is partly constructed by the imposition of concepts' (Devitt, 1991, p. 235).

But doing away with demarcation is not without its pitfalls either. While it might be true that there is scientific knowledge beyond what is objectively defined, the absence of demarcation leads to the assumption that all of science is subjective. This view clearly undermines the distinction between statements that are more likely to be objectively true and those that are less likely to be so. And providing the cloak of science to statements that are no more than subjective beliefs can be dangerous, especially in the social sciences. It can lead to distortions in the use of the authority of science. At one extreme it can lead to the authority of science being used to justify actions with even heinous social consequences, as happened under Stalin. At the other extreme, when it leads to complete relativism, it can erode the authority of science and equate statements based on a rational understanding with those that are completely irrational.

If these costs are to be avoided there is a need to retain a demarcation between the rational and the irrational. But the demarcation cannot be a constraint. It must allow for all possible influences on the growth of science. And if it is to be of any use to policy makers it must be possible to make it in the real world rather than in the abstract realm alone. For instance, Popper's distinction between falsifiability, as a logical concept, and falsification, as a set of rules may be a useful philosophical device. Most of the criticism would be against falsification rather than falsifiability. But for a policy maker interested only in the realm of actual rules, the distinction is not of very great significance.

An appropriate criterion for demarcation would have to overcome the twin risks of either being too narrow or too broad. When science is too narrowly defined it leaves out a large number of issues which a policy maker may have to legitimately deal with. As there are no norms to deal with such issues, there is considerable scope for expediency. At the other end, if science is too loosely defined, it allows for non-scientific statements to be considered scientific. This again allows for expediency. An effective methodology for economic policy makers must find a way of demarcating the scientific from the non-scientific that minimises the scope for expediency.

The need for such a demaraction is even greater in a method as inclusive as the Gandhian one. As it explicitly deals with both reason and faith, providing them different roles, it needs to demarcate the two. Gandhi's approach to demarcation runs parallel to that of Popper, up to a point. The distinction Gandhi makes between absolute and relative truth is quite consistent with Popper's views on truth and truthlikeness. Gandhi's contention that we must always function with the relative truth is also consistent with the Popperian view. Gandhi's demarcation between reason and faith can also be approximated to the demarcation Popper draws between science and metaphysics. Further, Gandhi's view that reason cannot be completely independent of faith is consistent with Popper's contention that he did not think it was possible to eliminate all 'metaphysical elements' from science.

It is in dealing with this weak demarcation that there are sharp differences between the approach of Popper and that of Gandhi. As someone operating primarily within the realm of philosophy, Popper's preoccupation was with the importance of this demarcation for scientific method. Even when he recognised the scope for the misuse of science in practice by presenting false theories as scientific, he tried to address the problem only from within the realm of science. His means of preventing authoritarian regimes from claiming the support of science was to define increasingly strict criteria for demarcation between science and non-science.

The Gandhian response to the weak demarcation between reason and faith is very different. As a practising politician he was not preoccupied with questions of scientific method alone. While the dividing line between reason and faith may well have been of interest to him, he had no reason to impose a precise dividing line when, in reality, the demarcation was much more blurred. Popper's practical concerns about preventing the use of science to justify oppression too evoked a very different response from Gandhi. As a contemporary of both Hitler and Stalin, Gandhi was quite aware of the consequences of a theory that was considered scientific being used for destruction. The Gandhian method thus stressed tolerance towards other points of view. And he was not constrained to meeting this challenge through a redefinition of the boundaries of science. He preferred to directly work against the use of science to justify killing, through his concept of *ahimsa* or non-violence.[10] He, therefore, did not feel the practical need to impose a stricter-than-desired demarcation between reason and faith which would constrain the inclusiveness of his method.

In defining this weak demarcation, the Gandhian method uses subjectivity in a way that is quite different from that of some other critics of Popper. For these critics the acceptance of subjectivity in science implies that there cannot be a clear demarcation. Knowledge must then be treated as one indivisible whole. Consequently, the very existence of subjective knowledge implies that it cannot be objective. In other words, knowledge can be either subjective or objective. Thus for Feyrabend, the very fact that something cannot be understood in objective terms alone is sufficient reason to accept the principle of anything-goes in the search for knowledge. For Gandhi on the other hand, the mere existence of subjectivity does not imply the absence of any need for demarcation between reason and faith. What it does do is recognise that this demarcation could itself have a subjective dimension.

This explicit role for the subjective in demarcation alters the perception of the problem. The difficulties with the demarcation criteria in the debate in the philosophy of science arise because the search has been restricted to objective criteria alone. The debate clearly brings out the limitations of such objective criteria. Both falsification and the test of predicting novel facts fail as perfect criteria to demarcate the rational from the rest. The Gandhian use of subjectivity addresses this problem by first reducing the costs of a misplaced demarcation. As there is a role for both reason and faith in the growth of knowledge, the costs of a wrong demarcation are not as serious as in methods that believe that reason alone should be considered.

A second effect of the inclusion of subjectivity is that it automatically rules out the possibility of one universal criterion or set of criteria. Different analysts would pick different criteria or sets of criteria. The Gandhian method would even allow for the same analyst to accept different betting quotients for different components of an action. For instance, there would be a core consisting of statements tested by the most rigorous of tests, say falsifiability, to which are attached the highest betting quotients. This could be surrounded by another area where statements come through less rigorous tests, like the ability to generate novel facts, which would have lower betting quotients. And then there could be another area where we can put statements that neither pass the test of falisifiability nor are able to generate novel facts, where the betting quotients are the least. The validity of these demarcations would itself be decided by the ability of the user to predict events.

DEALING WITH SUBJECTIVITY

Much of the attention paid to subjectivity in economics has been on predicting individual behaviour." Typically, subjective behaviour is sought to be explained in terms of rationality. And rationality, in turn, is reduced to specific elements such as consistency and maximising self-interest. These assumptions about subjective behaviour are not beyond being challenged, and have, in fact, been challenged by a number of eminent scholars. The weaknesses of dealing with subjectivity in this manner become even more obvious when discussing methodological issues. Surely no economist can argue that he must maximise self-interest when choosing the appropriate unit of analysis or the key factors that must be analysed. Not surprisingly, the approach to subjectivity in economic methodology has been somewhat different. They have tended to look at other dimensions of subjectivity. But these alternative approaches have not been adequate either. For a while, the question did not go very much beyond asking whether economics was a positive or a normative science.[12] When the question is posed in this form it can lose much of its relevance. Economics can have both positive and normative elements. There is a normative element in deciding which questions an economist must raise. Some of the specific answers the economist then works out, such as the relationship between demand and supply in a particular economy at a particular point of time, could be positively determined. Classifying economics as either a positive or a normative science could then be a largely meaningless exercise which would seem to deserve Irving Fisher's contempt for methodology.

This contempt may have been strong enough for economists to ignore methodological issues for a while. But these issues have refused to simply go away. Economists have found it necessary to ponder over the role of judgements in economic analysis from time to time. Even economists generally considered conservative, like John Hicks, have stressed the importance of judgement in economics (Hicks, 1979). These judgements can extend beyond the evaluation of evidence to identifying the factors needed to understand a specific situation. The choice of a specific unit of analysis could itself involve a significant judgement. In the *General Theory,* Keynes listed among the 'three perplexities that have most impeded my progress' (Keynes, 1983, p. 37), the choice of the appropriate unit to analyse a problem. Much of mainstream economics is thus caught between an unwillingness to consider the methodological implications of subjectivity and a recognition of the role that subjectivity inevitably plays in the practice of economics.

In contrast, the Gandhian method deals squarely with the methodological issues that are thrown up by subjectivity. Indeed, the most striking aspect of the Gandhian method's approach to subjectivity is that it does not seek to reduce it. It recognises that knowledge has both its subjective and objective dimensions, and both dimensions must be understood. While it recognises that subjectivity could lead to bias, it does not believe that the way to reduce bias is to reduce subjectivity. Instead, the focus of the Gandhian method is on improving the quality of subjective judgements. A biased judgement would then call for improvement in the use of subjectivity rather than believing that the role played by subjective judgements can be wished away.

The role of the subjective in the Gandhian method is perhaps better understood if we invoke Nagel's distinction between characterising value judgements and appraising value judgements. Characterising value judgements are evaluations of evidence, 'which conclude that a given characteristic is in some degree present (or absent) in a given instance' (Nagel, 1984, p. 492) and appraising value judgements are evaluations 'which conclude that some envisaged or actual state of affairs is worthy of approval or disapproval' (ibid., p. 493).

The Gandhian method seeks to improve the quality of both types of value judgements. The quality of appraising value judgements is to be improved primarily by ensuring consistency. Appraising value judgements would need to be consistent with a pre-defined morality. The appraising value judgements made on each of the elements of an action would also have to be consistent with each other.

Consistency is obviously essential for improving the quality of characterising value judgements as well. But it is not enough. Improving the quality of characterising value judgements also requires two apparently contradictory approaches. At one level, Gandhi advocates participant observation so that the policy maker can identify with the target of his policies. Such an identification is expected to provide a better understanding of conditions on the ground, which in turn would improve his or her characterising value judgements. At the same time, he also advocates a distancing of the analyst from the analysis so that there is no bias in the characterising value judgements. But, as has been noted earlier, the apparent contradiction disappears once we recognise the dominant role the method provides for consequentialism. The advocacy of non-attachment is to the consequences of an action. When the policy maker is completely unattached to the consequences of his action, his characterising value judgements are unlikely to be biased. Participant observation, on the other hand, is only to improve the formulation of an action, so that the characterising value judgements needed when formulating a policy benefit from greater awareness of local conditions. Ideally, participant observation would have to be carried out in a way that the policy maker gains no attachment, material or otherwise, to the consequences of his action.

THE CHALLENGE OF RHETORIC

The debate on economic methodology since the 1980s has focused attention on several specific elements of subjectivity in economic analysis. Prominent among these elements has been the rhetoric used by economists. The debate has generated wider recognition that the norms economists use when addressing each other make a difference to their ability to convince. A comprehensive understanding of an economist's perception then depends on an understanding of his or her rhetoric. Policy makers have for long been aware of the rhetorical value of words like 'reform'. In countries like India, 'reform' has been used, sometimes by the same policy makers at different times, to describe both a takeover by the state as well as privatisation.[13]

The role that Gandhi envisaged for rhetoric is among the less explored aspects of his method. Gandhi not only accepted rhetoric as one of the elements of knowledge, but also sought to explore its specific role. One of the elements of the inclusive concept of knowledge Gandhi borrowed from the Bhagvadgita was the distinction between the knower and the knowledge of the field. And understanding rhetoric was clearly one of the elements in this distinction. Gandhi clearly saw that rhetoric could play a role in analysis that was at least as important as the one envisaged by McCloskey.

Where Gandhi would have differed from McCloskey was in outlining the role that rhetoric should play. McCloskey tends to take a rather eclectic view of the need for such an analysis. As he sees it, 'The reasons to do a rhetorical analysis of an economic text are various: to understand it, to admire it, to debunk it, to set it beside other works of persuasion in science, to see that science is not a new dogma but is thoroughly and respectably part of the culture' (McCloskey, 1994, p. 336). As Uskali Maki points out, for 'McCloskey and those who agree with him, rhetorical persuasion is an activity directed towards raising (or, alternatively, lowering) the degree of plausibility of an economic theory or a statement about such a theory' (Maki, 1993b, pp. 23–24).

Such a view that accepts any change in the degree of plausibility is not consistent with the Gandhian method. The method's emphasis on consequentialism implies that even rhetoric has to be judged by the goodness of its consequences. In that sense the Gandhian method would be much closer to what Maki calls the realist alternative which views 'rhetorical persuasion, in addition [to changing the degree of plausibility], as an attempt to discover and communicate truths about the economy' (ibid., p. 24). Indeed, the Gandhian method can be said to go much further as it requires very much greater attention to be paid to the evaluation of rhetoric. The ability to identify the role of rhetoric is expected to improve the quality of judgements made while predicting specific consequences of actions. And when these predicted consequences are evaluated through the use of betting quotients, the role of rhetoric in these predictions will be a part of what is being evaluated.

Such a combined evaluation after the consequences are known may not be a sufficient guard against the misuse of rhetoric. Since the role of rhetoric falls outside the boundaries of rationality defined at a point of time, it is possible to use rhetoric to justify positions which have little chance of resulting in the desired consequences. This danger would be particularly great if there is a long gap between the action and the consequence. For instance, if the German people were aware of all the consequences of Nazism in the early 1930s itself, they may not have supported Hitler. But the relatively long period it took for the consequences to become evident, allowed greater room for the misuse of rhetoric.

For the Gandhian method, therefore, it is important not just to evaluate rhetoric but to also guard against its misuse. To the extent that this misuse can be conscious, it would depend on the importance given to ethical values. If ethics plays an important role in analysis, the conscious misuse of rhetoric would be minimised. This is one of the factors underlying Gandhi's belief that economics and ethics cannot be separated; that ethical values were essential for sound economics. But even if one does not consciously misuse rhetoric, it is still possible to misuse it in support of a belief that is false. Indeed, rhetoric itself could lead to belief in an idea that is false which could then lead to further exposition of that rhetoric. The extent of such subconscious misuse of rhetoric would depend, among other things, on whether a person evaluating an action has an interest in whether the action is accepted or not. The most unbiased evaluation would come from a person who has no interest in the consequences of the action. His non-attachment would extend to not just tangible consequences, but would also include the less tangible ones, like the vindication of the idea behind the action. Non-attachment thus becomes a critical factor in improving the quality of the evaluation. And if non-attachment is to extend to the idea behind the action, it would demand humility in the person evaluating the action. Humility is thus an essential requirement for a non-attached evaluation of the possible consequences of an action, and hence preventing the subconscious misuse of rhetoric.

THE ROLE OF INTERPRETATION

The debate on economic methodology has also stressed the need to understand issues like the role of subjectivity in interpretation. Consequently, there has been considerable interest in hermeneutics 'defined as the study of the interpretation of texts' (Gerrard, 1993, p. 51). The study of interpretation is particularly relevant for economic policy makers as the same theories can be interpreted in very different ways. Even something as well established as Keynes's *General Theory* is prone to quite diverse interpretations. This can be seen in the contrast between neo-Keynesian and Monetarist interpretations of Keynes. As Carabelli outlines the neo-Keynesian point of view:

> For Keynes, a monetary macroeconomy is a system characterised by 'complexity', possessing attributes such as organic independence among variables, non-homogeneity through time and space, non-numerical measurability, physical heterogeneity, openness, incompleteness, indivisibility, secondary qualities, contingency and change (Carabelli, 1992, pp. 3–4).

Monetarists on the other hand have a very different interpretation of the Keynesian system. Friedman, for instance, insists that:

> ... the heart of the General Theory is an extremely simple hypothesis—that a highly unstable marginal efficiency schedule of investment and a liquidity preference function that is highly elastic at low rates of interest and unstable at higher rates of interest are the key to short-run economic movements. That is what gives investment its central role, what makes the consumption function and the multiplier the key concepts, what enables Keynes to develop his theory for 165 pages without having to introduce the quantity of money (Friedman, 1972, p. 908).

Policy makers need to not only interpret old theories and evidence about specific situations, but they also need to understand how their actions may be interpreted by others. In the process of reforming economies, for instance, policy makers find themselves repeatedly confronted by the need to ensure the most desirable interpretation of their actions. The ability of reforming economies to attract capital depends on the investors' perception of their reforms. In advanced economies the role of interpretation may be even greater, as market-makers continuously interpret the likely impact of policy initiatives on the health of the economy.

Gandhi was extremely sensitive to the role of interpretation in developing an action. This sensitivity has now been documented. Tarlo's analysis of Gandhi's dress provides evidence of his sensitivity to the role of interpretation of not just what he said or wrote, but also of how he dressed (Tarlo, 1996). This sensitivity to interpretation was not accidental and was, in fact, internal to the Gandhian method. With the Gandhian method being based on the concept of knowledge in the Bhagvadgita, there is always an awareness of the role of interpretation. Since knowledge in the Gita is defined in terms of its specific elements, knowledge of the whole is based on knowledge of parts of the whole and knowledge of the parts is itself influenced by knowledge of the whole. There is thus a recognition of the need to address the hermeneutical circle, where interpreting a text requires pre-knowledge of the text. This circle is, however, not as much of a constraint for Gandhi as it would be for those seeking objectivity. For those seeking objectivity the circle would have to be broken so as to arrive at the absolute objective truth. Gandhi, on the other hand, believed that the absolute truth was an ideal towards which we could work but which would never be attained. And he recognised the role of subjectivity when working with relative truth. As such he only needed to enter the hermeneutical circle and his knowledge would keep growing with the knowledge of the parts improving his knowledge of the whole, which would in turn improve his knowledge of the parts. This approach is consistent with the view of Heidegger that what is decisive is not to get out of the hermeneutical circle but to come into it the right way (Gerrard, 1993).

For Gandhi, the right way to enter the hermeneutical circle was to seek to distinguish between the essential and the non-essential. As this ability would vary from person to person and over time, interpretations of the same situation could vary. The accuracy of an interpretation could be evaluated over time. This implies that the validity of an interpretation can only be decided after its effects are seen. And even then it may not be possible to accurately evaluate the quality of the interpretation, as it would form but one part of a larger action that is being evaluated. It is, therefore, important to develop safeguards against misinterpretation, whether deliberate or not. Just as there is a need to guard against the misuse of rhetoric there is a need to guard against the misuse of interpretation, either deliberately or subconsciously. And the same safeguards used in the case of rhetoric would be valid here as well. Interpretation would be among the inputs into an action that is evaluated when a betting quotient is judged by actual experience. But since the betting quotient is a reflection of the whole action, rather than its individual components, interpretation too needs other safeguards. And, as in the case of rhetoric, these safeguards are primarily provided by non-attachment to the consequences of an action.

METHOD OF INTERVENTION

Among the aspects of policy making that have received much less attention than they deserve in the debate on economic methodology is the relationship between the method of understanding an economy and the mechanism of policy implementation. In fact, the tasks of understanding an economy and that of implementing policy are often seen as two very different branches of economics. And yet the method of understanding the economy has a direct bearing on the mechanism of policy implementation. If we understand an economy by reducing it to a model, the policy instruments are also determined by that model. A model that provides a major role for money supply would justify using money supply as the main instrument of intervening in the economy. The unit described in the model will also be treated as the ideal unit of intervention. When these models seek to explain more than one aspect of the economy they can take on an ideological hue. This is most obvious in the case of all-encompassing theories, such as the Marxist models. But even relatively narrower models do tend to suggest specific methods of intervention across vastly different situations. Thus Monetarists tend to focus primarily on money supply, just as Keynesians focus on the adequacy of demand.

As the Gandhian method opposes the reduction of reality into a single model, its method of intervention in the economy is necessarily more pluralistic. Its focus on consequences makes it open to any instrument that is available at a point of time to achieve a particular consequence. Its inclusiveness implies that the analysis cannot be restricted to a few key factors, no matter how important they may be. As a corollary, the intervention in the economy cannot be through only a few select factors. And since the Gandhian method deals with a multiplicity of units of analysis, the intervention in the economy too would have to be at different levels of aggregation. In the Gandhian method, the system of regulation and policy implementation would operate at a multiplicity of levels, beginning with the local and going on to higher degrees of aggregation right up to the global. The movement from a lower degree of aggregation to a higher one would only be justified when the more decentralised unit cannot, for whatever reason, operate effectively. The Gandhian mechanism for intervention in the economy would then not be just a single macroeconomic agency. Instead, it would be a variety of agencies working together to develop as inclusive a picture of the economy as possible. The specific agencies that need to come together would vary from one desired consequence to another. The efficient utilisation of water might call for a group of agencies related to that river basin, while the efficient utilisation of power might call for a group of agencies that includes representatives of all the users of power.

The main advantage of such a pluralistic, flexible method of policy implementation is that it increases the instruments available to a policy maker. He does not have to rely on the market or the government machinery alone to intervene in the economy. There could be collective action to achieve a specific economic objective. Gandhi used his movement against foreign cloths as, among other things, a means of changing the conditions faced by Indian cloth manufacturers. In a more modern context too collective action has had some success in influencing demand patterns. Environmentalists have influenced a variety of economic factors including the fuel consumption of automobiles. But such changes have often been brought about through external pressure on policy makers. In the Gandhian method these pressures would be internalised into the mechanism of formulating and implementing policy. Groups such as the environmentalists would be an integral part of the process of formulating and implementing policy. This would serve to make these pressure groups more aware of the factors influencing others in the policy making process. Environmentalists, for instance, would be forced to also address factors other than the environment. And if the pressure groups do not get bureaucratised, they will provide policy makers with new instruments of policy implementation, such as collective action.

If this pluralism of policy instruments is not to lead to complete anarchy it is essential that policy makers are very sensitive to unintended consequences. Since the Gandhian method also recognises the fallibility of all knowledge, the implementation agency must be in a position to change course at the first sight of a policy developing unintended adverse consequences. A reform programme based on the Gandhian method would then begin gradually, with an extensive monitoring of unintended consequences. It is only when the unintended consequences are manageable and there is sufficient evidence of the measures leading to the desired consequences, that the momentum of the reform will be speeded up. The sensitivity to the fallibility of policy will also ensure that the focus will be on first alleviating the more extreme pain of a crisis, if need be through short term measures. And once the economy is in a position to absorb the shocks of unintended consequences, the necessary systemic changes will be brought about. The mechanism to implement a policy would thus be sensitive both to the need to reduce the possibility of error as well as the need to reduce the undesirable consequences of an error.

APPROACHES TO CONFLICT

One of the major challenges to a policy maker is to deal with conflicts of interest. The two most common approaches to conflict in the economy are not consistent with the Gandhian method. The first approach to a conflict of economic interests consists primarily of allowing the market to determine the relations between different economic interest groups.[14] In this approach the government steps in only when the market comes up with results that are not socially sustainable. A typical example of this approach would be the case where the market is given a free hand even if it generates inequality. The more extreme adverse effects of inequality are then addressed through a system of doles. The Gandhian method would, no doubt, appreciate the fact that the market offers many more economic options to individuals than a state dominated system. But providing a free hand to the market would go against two other tenets of the Gandhian method. First, in the process of balancing the economic power of different groups, the market ignores those who do not have economic power. If a person cannot afford to buy a product the market keeps him out. It is not the responsibility of a free market to ensure that all groups in society are empowered to benefit from it. Second, what is acceptable to the market need not necessarily meet broader social criteria of fairness. In its pure form the market has little concern for social factors. A price would be acceptable to a market if it balances the economic forces at play, even if it leads to increasing social inequalities and tensions.

Any attempt to offset the unfairness of the market through doles would also not always find favour with the Gandhian method. The consequentialism of the Gandhian method would reject any system of charities that leads to undesirable consequences. And the dependence of major sections of the poor in a society on doles, rather than the self-respect of work, is unlikely to be considered desirable.

The second major approach to conflict is based on the belief that the resolution of a conflict is only possible when the oppressed gain dominance over the existing ruling élite.[15] This approach can lead to a variety of specific theories depending upon the characterisation of the oppressed and the precise nature of the primary conflict. The Gandhian method's objection to this approach would be twofold. First, it would argue that it is often difficult to decide which is the primary conflict in a society. The same social situation can lead to more than one group laying claim to being the primary oppressed. In a typical situation in a developing country, is the working class, to be considered the oppressed or should that distinction go to other groups like the tribals? And clubbing groups of the oppressed is not easy as there could be conflicts between them. It could be in the interests of the working class to support, say, a large hydel power project that submerges the traditional habitat of the tribals. And when there are a large number of conflicts, as there tend to be in any complex society, there could be differences of opinion on which conflict should be considered the primary one in a society. To take the Indian example, even if we agree, for the sake of argument, that the Dalits constitute the entire oppressed, is the primary conflict in their economic relations or in their social relations? The answer to that question could decide who the oppressors are. This difficulty in arriving at a satisfactory comprehensive theory has, in fact, now gained wide recognition. It has even led some to go slow in the search for such a comprehensive theory. Pieterse, for instance, argues: 'The total theory and universal vision of emancipation may not be succeeded by another total theory, but by an awareness of plurality. There is no need to rush in the search for a new paradigm' (Pieterse, 1992, p. 28). While recognising plurality may be a sign of realism, it does not help us in choosing between competing theories. Without a theory that is widely accepted, rightly or wrongly, it would be difficult to justify removing one dominant group and replacing it with another.

The second Gandhian objection to the resolution of a conflict through the oppressed vanquishing the oppressors relates to the consequences of such an approach. Even if there is a broad unanimity on the nature of oppression, as sometimes seemed to be the case at the height of the appeal of communism, focusing on the oppressed alone would go against the basic tenets of the Gandhian method. The inclusiveness of the method implies that no perspective of policy implementation based on one section of society alone would be acceptable. Even when the majority is oppressed the resolution of the conflict cannot be based on the overthrow and then oppression of the former élite. And the violence, which would more often than not be involved in the overthrow of one group by another, would go against the basic requirement of the Gandhian method that the actions must be good in themselves.

Rather than leaving conflict to be resolved entirely through the power of the oppressed or the objectivity of the free market, the Gandhian method would seek to resolve a conflict through a bargained consensus. In order to improve the quality of the bargained consensus, the method would work towards increasing the options available, empowering the weak and establishing clear norms of fairness. To achieve these objectives the method would be open to using a diverse set of instruments. It could use the market to provide more options. It could then use the power of the state to empower the economically backward. It could use collective action as well as advertising to increase awareness and establish norms of fairness. It is only when these instruments come into direct conflict with each other that a choice would have to be made between, say, a free market and state intervention.

* * *

The focus of the Gandhian method on action thus provides a framework that is inclusive in methodological terms as well. It covers the entire range of activities that go into the implementation of a policy action right from the underlying theoretical understanding to the final act of policy implementation. Such an inclusive view alters the parameters of the debate on economic methodology. When seen from the inclusive perspective of the Gandhian method, it becomes clear that not all participants in the debate are addressing the same issues. Some, like supporters of Popper's falsificationism, are more concerned with factors involved in the rational component of knowledge, while others, like those concentrating on rhetoric and interpretation, tend to emphasise the influences on faith. And yet others, like the followers of Kuhn. are interested in the changing boundaries of rationality through history. Thus, far from being the mutually exclusive explanations of all knowledge that they are sometimes portrayed to be, each of the contributions are really dealing with different components of knowledge. Conventional wisdom may demand that the acceptance of Popper's falsificationism must necessarily mean rejecting the role for history that Kuhn visualised as well as the role of rhetoric as argued by McCloskey. But in the Gandhian system there could be a set of propositions where a rigorously defined rational system, such as falsificationism, prevails. This body of propositions would grow through history as we move from one relative truth to another, whether it follows the pattern that Kuhn postulated for scientific revolutions or any other. And beyond what is considered rational at any point of time would be factors like rhetoric or interpretation that influence the faith an individual has in a particular proposition. It is then quite possible for Popper's ideas to dominate the rigorous set of propositions that can be considered rational at any point of time, even as Kuhn's perception of history determines how this set of rationally determined propositions will change over time and McCloskey's ideas of rhetoric influence the faith in a set of propositions.

NOTES

1. For the concept of original position see Rawls (1971).
2. For the case for deontological consequentialism see Sen (1988).
3. For a summary of some recent trends in economic methodology see Backhouse (1994).
4. Much of the debate on economic methodology since 1980 has, in fact, focused on redefining in the context of economics issues that had been previously raised in debates in the philosophy of science.

5. For an elaboration of this criticism of economic models see, for instance, Ormerod (1994).
6. It could be argued that the attempt to mix the free market with state control was not intrinsic to the Indian second plan model. It was a two-sector model in which it was assumed that the state could control the key variables. It was just that in implementation one of the sectors, basic industry, was to be dominated by the state, while the other sector, consumer goods, was to be primarily controlled by the private sector.
7. It has been argued that the new theories need not be better theories, as it is quite possible that we could, over time, go back to an earlier theory as being better. But to the extent that the number of facts known increases over time, the new theories are better to the extent that they are not falsified by a larger number of facts. An old theory that returns in the face of a larger number of facts will then have greater credibility than it had in its earlier incarnation.
8. A similar view is held by Hands: 'Popperian philosophy of science has been extremely influential in economic methodology. Popperian "falsificationism", first introduced into economics by Hutchison (1938), remains one of the dominant approaches to economic methodology. In addition to this direct influence, Popperian philosophy has also affected economic methodology through the work of Imre Lakatos. A fairly extensive literature has developed around the question of the applicability of Lakatos's "methodology of scientific research programmes" (MSRP) to economies' (Hands, 1993, p. 61).
9. For an effective summary see Blaug (1980).
10. For an exposition of Gandhi's use of non-violence and a comparison with Martin Luther King, see Dalton (1998).
11. This behaviour has, in turn, been largely defined in terms of rationality. As Sen argues, 'The assumption of "rational behaviour" plays a major part in modern economics. Human beings are assumed to behave rationally, and given this special assumption, characterising rational behaviour is not, in this approach, ultimately different from describing actual behaviour' (Sen, 1988, pp. 10–11).
12. The origins of the debate on the positive and normative aspects of economics can be traced at least as far back as Lionel Robbins's seminal work, *An Essay on the Nature and Significance of Economic Science*. See Robbins (1984).
13. Even after the coming of liberalisation the term agrarian reform in India was still associated with state intervention, including the state taking over surplus land.
14. This group would include not only those who seek an unfettered free market, but also those who would like a market led approach with the state intervening only in times of extreme distress.
15. The foremost among these theories are those based on class conflict. But there can be variations of this perception that deal with conflicts between other social groups. In the Indian context, there have been theorists like Lohia or Ambedkar who focused on conflict between castes.

5

Departure from Convention

In our outline of the Gandhian method we have been guided primarily by the requirements of the policy maker. It is, for instance, the policy maker's compulsion to act that increases the attractiveness of the primacy of action in the Gandhian method. This must not, however, give the impression that any policy maker does, or even should, go through the entire set of methodological issues before determining policy. It is very unlikely that a policy maker will always have the time, even if he has the inclination, to do so. Instead, policy makers tend to operate on the basis of conventional norms. Several of these norms have their roots in the debates on methodology. The policy maker's emphasis on falsifiability when using data to evaluate a situation, for one, can be traced to the Popperian dominance in economics. But the link between conventions and method is not always as clear. There are times when the power of conventional wisdom is so overwhelming that individuals accept conventions that are derived from ideologies they do not support. The most striking example is the relationship between falsification and some Marxist empirical studies. One of the objectives of Popper's development of falsification was to challenge Marxism. Yet it is not unknown for Marxist economists in their empirical work to adhere strictly to falsification. Again, the link between conventions and method can also be blurred by limitations of the method itself. For instance, we have already noted the ambivalence in the Popperian method towards the choice of the questions to be asked. Consequently, the questions to be raised could be decided just by the existing conventions. If the convention is to identify issues only after they have reached crisis proportions, it is the crisis that will determine the questions that are raised. No analysis of the method of policy makers is then complete without evaluating the relationship between that method and existing conventions. And when the method is different from the one underlying existing norms, it calls for a departure from convention.

To make a comprehensive list of all the conventions followed by economists is a daunting task. These conventions could relate to a whole variety of issues. The conventions could relate to the unit of analysis. Most economists tend to focus primarily on national economies. The conventions could relate to the measures of success. Most economists tend to treat growth as a primary indicator of economic success. There are even conventions on the role of individuals. A firm, for instance, is generally treated as an individual entity, rather than as a collection of individuals. The number of conventions would increase further if we take into account the variations that exist across countries. Some countries, even after the collapse of communism, tend to rely a lot more on state intervention than others. A comprehensive list of all conventions along with an analysis of how the Gandhian method either endorses or departs from them is thus a huge task, well beyond the scope of this exercise. All that we intend to do here is to identify some of the major conventions that the Gandhian method abandons.

THE NATIONAL ECONOMY

The most striking, and fundamental, challenge the Gandhian method poses to the conventional in macroeconomics is, arguably, in the role of the national economy. In conventional economics the national economy is the focus of all analysis. The very success or failure of the economy is measured in terms of the growth, or otherwise, of its gross national product (GNP). A country with a high GNP is considered developed even if there are some local economies within it where conditions remain backward. The management of the economy too concentrates on national macroeconomic parameters such as the overall rate of inflation. Runaway inflation in one small pocket of the economy would not merit much attention unless it reaches proportions where it affects the national picture, either by making an impact on the overall rate of inflation or by causing sufficient distress to merit national attention. The points of intervention in the economy are also largely national, though the extent of the preoccupation with the national does vary from country to country. In India, for instance, one of the most important instruments of intervention in agriculture has, for many years, been nationally decided procurement prices.[1]

Even when dealing with the global or sub-national dimensions of economics, the focus remains on the national economy.[2] International trade is analysed in terms of its impact on national economies. Indeed, during the Uruguay round negotiations that led to the creation of the WTO, countries adopted positions on global trade rules based on their perception of national interests. Global financial crises too are addressed more by national governments than by international financial organisations.[3] Within the nation too it is conventional to treat local economies as no more than components of a national economy. Where the interests of the local economy and the national economy come into conflict, it is generally the interests of the national economy that prevail. To cite a common example, the local environmental costs of a project are generally treated as acceptable if they are outweighed by gains to the national economy.[4]

The Gandhian method's approach to the national economy is much more multidimensional. As it does not need to reduce reality to a single model, it does not confine itself to the unit of analysis associated with that model. Its unit of analysis need not be restricted to either the firm or the national economy. It can choose any unit, from the village or firm to the national and global, depending on what is most appropriate to address the issues concerned. And even when the issue calls for a national focus, the analysis will not be confined to the national economy alone. This is evident if we break up the Gandhian method into two stages. In the first stage, when the desirable consequences are chosen, the principle of Swadeshi ensures that the focus is entirely on the relevant local economy. For issues where the appropriate unit of analysis is the national, the relevant local economy would be the national economy. This would be true, for instance, of questions relating to regional trade blocs and international trade. In the second stage, the method identifies the actions that can bring about these desirable consequences as well as the unintended consequences of these actions. At this stage, the exercise is thrown open to consider all possible dimensions whether it is at the level of the sub-national, national or global economies. Thus while the national picture is obviously important, economies cannot be viewed from the national perspective alone. The national economy should, to use Boulding's term, be 'desacrilized' (Boulding, 1992, p. 227).

Such a multidimensional approach has its impact on policy choices. For instance, when the focus is on the national economy, strategies to control inflation concentrate almost entirely on specific macroeconomic variables like the fiscal deficit or interest rates. Local factors influencing prices, such as local supply bottlenecks, are largely ignored. The extent of the impact of local factors is, in fact, easy to underestimate. It is not necessary that a sharp, but localised, impact on prices must show up in the national picture of a large economy. In the national price index, the high prices in one pocket could be offset by a glut in another pocket. It is thus possible that even when national indices point to price stability there could be consumers in some pockets facing severe inflationary pressure and producers in other pockets facing the opposite problem of excess inventories. Conventional economics would brush aside these difficulties first with the assumption of perfect mobility of inputs and output; and then by arguing that if such perfect mobility does not exist, the economy must move towards it. But in large countries, particularly the more backward ones, the mobility of both inputs and output can be a serious bottleneck that cannot be easily overcome.

By recognising the multiplicity of economic units, the Gandhian method ensures that the strategy to fight inflation cannot be based on national level macroeconomic tools alone. As the desired consequence would be to reduce inflationary pressure on individuals or groups in each part of the economy, it cannot confine the analysis to factors influencing the national economy, like the fiscal deficit or interest rates. All factors influencing prices, including supply bottlenecks and demand patterns in the local economy, would need to be taken into account. As the method does not ignore the national or international dimensions either, it will provide a more comprehensive picture of inflation. In large backward economies, where the mobility of both input and output is poor, it will provide a greater role for local factors. In the more developed economies, on the other hand, with near-perfect mobility of input and output, the role of local factors may be marginal.

The focus on the local consequences could also alter methods of evaluating specific policy options. In conventional economics, issues like that of protection for individual industries are decided at the national level. Protectionist measures typically take the form of tariff or non-tariff barriers built for the national economy. The evaluation of whether an industry requires protection is thus done at the level of the nation as a whole. If an industry, in the nation as a whole, is losing out to global competition, there is pressure to protect that industry. The focus on the local economy in the Gandhian method fundamentally alters the approach to this issue. Whether an industry needs protection or not would be decided at the local rather than the national level. The protection that is required may not only be against foreign companies or imports, but also against national monopolies. Protection would then take the form of not just tariff barriers but also a competition policy. The criteria to judge the appropriate degree of protection would once again be the consequences for the local economy. In other words, protection would be justifiable if it has an overall positive effect on the ability of the local population to earn as well as consume. An industry would lose its case for protection if the cost to the consumers is so great as to outweigh the net benefits to its employees. This approach should normally ensure that protection for inefficient firms would be more the exception than the rule.

The effect of a multidimensional approach, rather than a purely national one, would be felt in the international sphere as well. The conventional approach to international economic issues is to evaluate them in purely national terms. This was probably always true, but has become even more evident with the ideological conflict between the socialist bloc and the advanced capitalist world receding into the background. Implicit in this approach is the view that an analysis of global issues based on national interests has an element of permanence about it. This is particularly true when the norms for the working of international fora are sought to be influenced in a way that suits national interests. But, in reality, there is no permanence to national interests. These interests can, in fact, change over time. Distorting international fora in a way that suits national interest at one point of time could result in the same fora working against the same nation, when its interests have changed. For instance, a country may support a dominant role for regional trade blocs in international trade if it is in a position to benefit from such a regionalisation of trade. But over time, protecting the market within a trade bloc may not be enough. It would then be necessary to lower barriers set up in other trade blocs. The bias in the global institutions in favour of protected trade blocs will then work against the interests of the country that helped create this bias. Change in a country's interests may not also be a long drawn out process. The direct consequences of an action designed to benefit a country may work against it if other countries follow suit. The obvious example is competitive devaluation of currencies. A devaluation carried out in isolation may help a country increase its exports, but after other countries have also devalued their currencies, the first country may be left with its original level of exports. In that case it would only have lost, as the value of its exports would have decreased with the quantity remaining the same. Thus distorting global institutions or policies in order to suit national interest can easily be counterproductive.

These weaknesses would not apply to an approach derived from an effective use of the Gandhian method. As the method uses a multiplicity of units of analysis, there can be no justification for international mechanisms being determined on the basis of national interests. Just as national interests require national institutions, international institutions have to be determined by international interests. Truly democratic international institutions would leave little scope for distortion by national interests. And such independent international institutions would, ideally, have the power to prevent mutually destructive actions, like competitive devaluations.

THE INSTITUTIONAL FRAMEWORK

The differences between the Gandhian method and conventional economics in their attitude to the national economy has a fallout on their perceptions of the ideal institutional framework. While the actual institutional framework at any point of time may be the result of a variety of forces, it is possible to identify an ideal institutional framework that is most consistent with a particular perception of an economy. Policy makers who focus on the national economy would prefer to have power concentrated at the national level. In the vertical hierarchy of institutions from the local to the global, the national institutions would be the most important. It would be these national institutions that determine the distribution of power at each level of aggregation. And the national institutions would find such a hierarchy easier to control, if there is a dominant institution at each level of aggregation. A focus on the national economy thus tends to support an institutional framework which is dominated by national institutions and which tends to further concentrate power in a few institutions at each level of aggregation.

Such a linear institutional framework does not suit the Gandhian method for at least two reasons. First, it does not have the flexibility the Gandhian method demands. The Gandhian method recognises that the appropriate unit of policy making would vary from issue to issue. The efficient use of river waters calls for an institution to determine policy for the entire river basin. A policy for the development of a particular language, on the other hand, calls for an institution that covers all the areas where that language is spoken. If these two areas do not coincide, and there is no reason why they always should, it would not be appropriate to have a single institution to handle both problems. Second, such a hierarchical institutional framework would not suit the Gandhian method's mechanism for resolving conflicts of interest between different local economies. The dominance of the national economy would result in national institutions taking on the responsibility for resolving differences between local economies. This would not provide room for local economies to arrive at a bargained consensus among themselves.

The ideal institutional framework for the Gandhian method would then be one of a large number of decentralised completely autonomous institutions. These local institutions would take up all the issues affecting the local economy that can be addressed locally. This would include the choice of desirable consequences as well as the actions towards these consequences that can be carried out locally. In addition, it would consider the unintended local consequences.

But these local institutions cannot work in isolation. As they interact with each other and the world outside, they would need larger institutions to govern their mutual interests. A macroeconomic strategy for, say, a river basin would be more efficient in the utilisation of water than individual local communities operating in isolation. These larger institutions could also provide the mechanism for bargained consensus among their members.

The precise boundaries of each of these larger institutions could vary from issue to issue. One set of local economies would get together to create an institution for an entire river basin. Each of these local economies would, however, remain free to join other groupings for, say, the development of their language. The appropriate levels of aggregation could also vary across regions and over time. Indeed, as the emergence of the Euro has shown, an element, such as a currency, that is considered national in one part of the world, can easily be treated as something requiring common action across several countries in another part of the world.

This flexible institutional framework would be relevant to all levels of aggregation. At the international level, each country would need the flexibility to join different groups according to the issues involved. Rather than become members of rigid blocs of the kind that dominated the world before the collapse of communism in Europe, each country would be a member of a variety of international groups, from groups of commodity producers to groups sharing common security interests. That is to say, the Gandhian method would not seek to replace the bipolar world with alternative alignments. Instead, it would seek to create a large number of genuinely autonomous international institutions, each committed to a specific dimension of the international situation.

The main advantage of this Gandhian institutional framework is that it allows for a bargained consensus at all levels of aggregation. Such a bargained consensus would ensure that when one economy bears the costs of the development of another, it would get a share of the benefit. In other words, when one local economy has to bear the costs of the development of another local economy, the benefits have to be transferred in a way that the economy bearing the costs believes it has not just been adequately compensated, but has benefited from the development. Actions that are not beneficial enough to provide for such a transfer of benefits would not be considered viable. The choice of specific benefits that must be transferred, and their magnitude, would be decided through a process of bargaining which is fair.

This approach would be equally valid for all levels of aggregation, from aggregating the interests of individuals in a local economy to aggregating the interests of regional blocs in a global economy. Local economies which together form a part of, say, a river basin would need to arrive at arrangements whereby the economies bearing the costs of development would be able to get a share of the benefits. Farmers whose lands are submerged by a hydel project, for instance, should have a stake in the power that is generated and sold from that project. Again, there can be a conflict between the river basin economy and the nearby metropolis over, say, environmental issues. The metropolitan economy would then have to pay for the damage to the environment at a rate that does not merely cover the costs to the present and future generations in the river basin. The metropolitan economy must also transfer sufficient benefits to the river basin for the population in the basin to desire the change. Similar examples can be worked out at the national, regional and global levels. Indeed, several principles that have been worked out independently of the Gandhian method would find a place in it. An obvious example of a norm that has been worked out independent of the Gandhian method but is consistent with it is the principle that 'the polluter must pay'.

It may not be practical to expect such an ideal institutional framework to emerge in any real situation. The best of intentions cannot guarantee that the delineation of the jurisdiction of each institution will be perfect in every part of the world. If nothing else, what is considered perfect may change over time as knowledge increases. Creating perfectly democratic institutions, where every individual's interests are given just the right importance, could also border on the impossible. But having identified an ideal it should be possible to judge whether an institutional framework is moving towards or away from that ideal. It is possible that institutions may be moving towards democratisation even when that is not the explicitly stated goal. The regionalisation of the global economy, for instance, would be a step towards democratisation of the global institutions if it leads to greater attention being paid to the interests of the smaller members of regional blocs. These smaller members may not, however, have been the driving force behind the creation of the bloc.

THE PREOCCUPATION WITH GROWTH

Another major departure from convention in the Gandhian method is in the attitude to growth. In the choice of objectives for economic policy it is conventional to provide the pride of place to growth. Economic policy makers may begin with a variety of objectives, but invariably most, if not all, of these objectives are believed to be captured in a single variable: growth. There have been efforts within conventional economics to counter the excessive emphasis on growth. Those concerned with the effects of growth have tended to emphasise the importance of distribution. And others concerned with the use of growth as an indicator of success have suggested broader indices like the human development index. But these efforts have remained on the periphery of economics. It is still conventional to look at growth as the best indicator of economic success. Economies, whether local, national or global, are considered successful if they achieve high growth rates, even if the growth makes no significant difference to major sections of the population. And the debate about growth versus distribution has, after the collapse of the communist world, largely given way to the belief that growth must precede distribution.

In contrast, the consequentialism of the Gandhian method does not encourage such a preoccupation with any single objective, including growth. The focus of the method is on identifying and achieving a set of desired consequences. These consequences in turn are defined in terms of an individual or groups of individuals in a local economy. The growth of the local, sub-national, national, regional or global economy can then only be a factor that helps achieve the desired consequence; it can only be a means to an end rather than an end in itself. If, say, the removal of poverty in a particular local economy is the desirable consequence, economic growth would certainly be one of the elements that would help achieve that consequence. But not much importance will be given to growth that does not lead to the removal of poverty.

The Gandhian method is thus very much more sensitive to non-growth objectives. The consequences desired by the local people in a local economy may not be based merely on increasing the production of commodities. It could also be based on greater consumer satisfaction from what is already produced. Take, for instance, the development of infrastructure. The emphasis would be as much on improved utilisation of existing infrastructure as on creating new infrastructure. There could even be cases where a unit saved would be more important than an additional unit produced. The obvious example is the power sector. An additional unit generated will make less than one unit available to the consumer because of transmission and distribution losses. As conservation saves power at the point of consumption, the benefit of the whole of the additional unit saved will be available to the consumer.

Among the other non-growth consequences desired by those belonging to a local economy is the removal of bottlenecks to distribution. Food shortages are often not so much the result of inadequate production as of non-availability of food where it is needed the most. If the non-availability is due to a lack of purchasing power, growth could be a necessary condition to achieve this objective. But it would not be sufficient. Growth must result in an increase in the purchasing power of those who face the brunt of the food shortage.

The emphasis on non-growth objectives brings the Gandhian method closer to some trends in mainstream economics that emphasise human development over growth. The human development index does cover a wide range of factors, some or all of which could be among the desired consequences of several local economies. But if the choice of factors taken into the index and their respective weightage were to be treated as anything more than a broad indicator for comparisons across economies, it would again go against the Gandhian method. In this method, the choice of desired consequences by the local population is supreme. Any consequences, howsoever lofty they may seem to those outside the local community, should not be forced on the local economy unless the local community itself desires it. Thus in the choice of objectives itself the Gandhian method would spread its net much wider than conventional economics.

CONSEQUENCES VERSUS KEY FACTORS

Another significant point of departure of the Gandhian method from conventional economics is its focus on consequences.

Conventional economic policy makers may start with a set of objectives that are comparable to the desired consequences of the Gandhian method. But they then, typically, go on to identify the main measures that would achieve these consequences. The focus then shifts to these actions, ignoring the others. It does not take long then for the emphasis to shift to a set of actions, completely ignoring the interaction between these actions and their consequences. Take, for example, the reform of the power sector in a developing economy. Conventional economic policy makers would set out with the objective of increasing the availability of power to consumers. They would then recognise that the main factor contributing to this availability is the generation of power. The emphasis would then be on increasing generation. If the government does not have the resources to do so, the emphasis would be on inviting private capital both from within the country and outside. And in order to do so the policy makers will be willing to offer substantial concessions.

It is quite easy to see that this strategy could go wrong in several ways. The concessions that are offered may be attractive individually but may become self-defeating in a macroeconomic context. If the real estate market is doing well, it may be attractive to a company to be offered more land than it needs. But if a series of such concessions leads to the supply of real estate outstripping demand, prices would crash. Again, the concessions could take the form of guaranteed offtake of power. This concession may seem inexpensive to the government in a situation of huge power deficits. But if it attracts sufficient projects, the government could find itself paying for power it cannot use. Yet again, the preoccupation with the main factor could also go wrong. The focus on generation could lead to ignoring the problems of the distribution of power. In which case the distribution system may not be able to take the additional power generated to the consumer.

These risks would be minimised in the Gandhian method. It too would begin with the desired objective of increasing the availability of power. But the emphasis on consequences will ensure that the focus will never shift away from this desired objective. It would consider all aspects of increasing the availability of power, from generation to distribution to conservation. It would then be geared to spotting any imbalance that may emerge, such as the costs of buying power that is not needed.

ABSORBING SPECIALISATION

The unwillingness of the Gandhian method to reduce reality to a set of key factors also ensures that its approach to specialisation is very different from the conventional. Conventional economics places a great deal of emphasis on specialisation. What may have begun as a simple division between macroeconomics and microeconomics is today a combination of a very much larger number of specialised fields. This is not to suggest that economists are unaware of the interlinkages between different specialised fields. But it is conventional to first study each field alone and then look for possible interlinkages. Where the linkages do not make a significant difference they are ignored. Economists who support controlling prices through the supply of money will agree that, say, transport bottlenecks could also influence prices; but they will insist that that influence is not so significant as to make a difference to the final result. There is then little reason to consider the links between monetary economics and transport economics. It is clear that in this approach additional factors are considered only if they are significant in themselves. And since the actual significance of a factor will only be known after the event, factors that become significant for the first time will necessarily be missed. Thus while this method helps gain in-depth knowledge it lacks a breadth of vision.

The absence of adequate attention to linkages can also influence the nature of questions that are raised. Often an approach that concentrates on the linkages between different aspects of an issue can come up with a totally different set of questions from an approach that relies on specialised efforts. For instance, a specialised approach to the economy of a less developed country would have a role for specialists in agriculture and specialists in industry. Policies would then be focused on the relationship between the two sectors as measured through indices like the terms of trade between agriculture and industry. Such an approach, however, completely ignores the possibility of there being a long term goal to move a major proportion of the population from agriculture to industry in a way that is least painful in economic, social and political terms. In fact, it is quite conceivable that in order to keep the terms of trade equitable, policy may actually be working towards keeping prices higher in agriculture. In such a situation, the policy would serve to keep people underemployed in agriculture rather than move them towards more efficient alternatives in industry.

The Gandhian method's attitude to specialisation is determined by its emphasis on linkages. As the method is based on the understanding that each consequence is also another action having its own consequences, it cannot ignore linkages. Even linkages that are minor in themselves could have a significant effect on the set of action-consequence relationships that make up the economy. While the depth of understanding provided by specialisation is undoubtedly desirable, it cannot come at the cost of ignoring linkages between different segments of the economy. Indeed, the emphasis that the Gandhian method places on dynamic linkages would guard against an inefficient, segmented conceptualisation of the economy.

A break from excessive specialisation can not only alter the answers to some specific questions, but can also raise new questions. For instance, does the growth of the information superhighway imply a shift in demand from products that cater to physical needs towards products that cater to needs of the intellect? If this is indeed the case, does it imply greater attention must be paid to issues such as the mental health of a society or the attractiveness of spiritualism? Even without the compulsions of dealing with a flood of intellectual products, Gandhi recognised the importance of such issues.

THE IDEOLOGICAL DIVIDE

It is conventional when analysing macroeconomic policy to divide the policy options on ideological lines.[5] Traditionally these options have been classified broadly as Right or Left, with the Right generally preferring a free market and the Left, state intervention. The precise dividing line between Right and Left is not always clear. There can be divisions within the Right or within the Left. Monetarists are only one group within the Right, just as Leninists are just one group within the Left. And there are groups that are considered a part of the Right by some and as part of the Left by others. Some Marxists would consider Keynesians as part of the Right, while for many Monetarists, Keynesians are a part of the Left. But this lack of clarity on the precise dividing line has not prevented economists from using the Left versus Right classification. It has only led to the identification of a series of positions from the extreme Left to the extreme Right. A policy option can then be placed anywhere on this scale depending on the extent to which it supports a free market or state intervention.

The convention of positioning policies against this backdrop has influenced the approach to Pragmatism as well. Pragmatism is seen as the willingness to pick up policy options from across the ideological spectrum. The scope that this approach offers for expediency typically does not receive much attention. It is assumed that the sole reason for choosing policies from different ideological frameworks is that it is pragmatic to do so. The detachment of individual policies from their ideological moorings also influences the relationship between the economics and politics of Pragmatism. As economic policies are not expected to fit into a predetermined ideological package, pragmatic political leadership is expected to give economic policy makers a relatively free hand. In principle at least, the theory is that there need be no connection between economics and politics. Thus a pragmatic Indian Prime Minister, Narasimha Rao, initiated economic reform by handing over the finance ministry to a technocrat, Dr Manmohan Singh. In China, Deng Xiao Ping refused to link his economic liberalisation to political reform.

In the Gandhian framework it is the method that is important, and not any ideological theory. The focus is on consequences rather than any specific theories. The Gandhian method would be open to consider alternative theories to achieve a particular consequence, if one set of theories fails. There cannot then be a commitment to any specific ideological theory. Moreover, the tendency to treat most problems as a choice between the market and the state goes against the inclusiveness of the Gandhian method. The market and the state are just two of the many instruments available to intervene in the economy. For instance, the intervention in the economy could occur through social institutions. The activities of a religious institution, such as opening schools, could very well influence the economy of a region. Social institutions could also influence the social behaviour of an individual. And since the Gandhian method focuses on the consequences to an individual in a local society, these influences could, at times, be very much more important than either the state or the market. This would be particularly true of remote, say tribal, economies where neither the state nor the market has penetrated. But even in more modern economies there are dimensions of economic behaviour that are influenced by institutions other than the state or the market. The attitude to specific ethnic groups, for instance, could well determine the role they play in the economy. It is for this reason that Gandhi remained largely outside the capitalism-versus-socialism debate that dominated global thinking in his time.

The distance between the Gandhian method and ideological theories may suggest a proximity to Pragmatism. The pragmatic policy maker too does distance himself from ideological positions. But pragmatists and followers of the Gandhian method would adopt very different approaches to functioning with a plurality of instruments. The focus of pragmatists would remain on a core set of policy instruments, which are extended to include instruments drawn from conflicting ideological models.[6] This is an add-on pluralism where the focus remains on the policy instruments that already dominate conventional economic thinking. The Gandhian method, on the other hand, starts from the other end. It begins with inclusiveness and seeks to use all instruments, big and small, known and previously unknown, to achieve the desired consequences. It would not be satisfied with intervening in the market or through state control; it would also consider other options such as collective action. The precise package of instruments it chooses will vary from situation to situation. Policy instruments that generally have only a minor impact could have an important role in specific situations due to the interaction of a variety of factors.

The Gandhian method would also differ from Pragmatism in its attitude to politics. It would not share the pragmatic economic policy maker's disdain for politics. The effectiveness of the bargaining in the policy making process of the Gandhian method will depend on the nature of the political and social systems. It is quite conceivable that each of the institutions at the local, sub-national, national, regional and global levels could end up defending specific vested interests rather than the interests of all whom they are supposed to represent. This distortion could take several forms, from global institutions being dominated by a few major powers to local institutions being dominated by a local feudal elite. In such unequal situations bargaining would be far from fair. The ideal Gandhian institutional framework thus requires not just perfect delineation of jurisdiction but also the effective empowerment of all the interests involved. An effective democratic system is then a necessary, though not sufficient, condition for effective empowerment. And this cannot be achieved if the policy maker ignores politics.

THE INDIVIDUAL AND THE FIRM

The challenge posed by the Gandhian method to conventional practices is as substantial in microeconomics as it is in macro-economic analysis. At the very outset it is conventional in microeconomics to treat the unit it is analysing as a homogenous entity. This homogenous entity can have no conflicts of interest within it. This is a reasonable enough assumption when the unit is an individual. An individual should be able to decide whether a development has a positive or a negative impact on him. Even when a development has both positive and negative effects, he should be in a position to decide whether, overall, the development is in his interests. It is when the assumption of homogenous interests is taken to the level of the firm that it becomes less reasonable. A firm involves a collection of individuals whose interests may not always coincide. Any specific objective a firm is expected to follow, say profit maximisation, need not always be in the interests of all those who are involved in the firm. Workers could believe that their interests are better served by a no-profit-no-loss objective. Indeed, there could be situations where it is not in the interests of even the owners of the firm for it to maximise its profits. Take the case of an individual who owns two firms, one producing an input and the other the final good. If the ad valorem tax on the input is higher than the tax on the final good, it would, other things remaining the same, be in the owner's interest to underprice the inputs and shift the profits to the final good. In such a situation the firm producing the input will not be maximising its profits.

The Gandhian method avoids this pitfall by focusing on the individual. The firm is seen as a collective of individuals. The firm cannot have a homogenous and independent identity as the interests of the different individuals within a firm need not necessarily coincide. The diversity would be even greater when these interests are influenced by the relationship between the individuals in the firm and conditions outside it. An owner's expectations from a firm are bound to be influenced by his interactions outside the firm. It could depend not just on his overall portfolio of investments but also on his social and political relations. And these interactions could follow a wide range of patterns. A criminal could see his firm as a means of gaining respectability. A philanthropist may decide he must maximise profits in order to have greater resources for his philanthropy. A worker's objectives in a firm could also depend on his relations outside the firm. A budding professional trade unionist may see the firm as no more than a base for him to build his support. The goals of a firm cannot then be defined independent of the goals of the individuals associated with it. The goals that are finally chosen for a firm will be the end result of bargaining between all who have a stake in it. Even when a firm is seen to represent only one interest, such as that of the owner, it does not mean that there are no other interests involved. All that it implies is that the other groups are not in a position to protect their interests.

Implicit in this concept is the view that the control of a firm cannot be fully understood in terms of the interests of any single group. Conventional microeconomics identifies control primarily with ownership. When the objective of a firm is said to be profit maximisation, for instance, it is assumed that what suits the owners suits those who control a firm. But control over a firm can, in reality also be influenced by other groups. In the days of trade union dominance it was not impossible for the unions to influence the goals a firm set for itself. Again, in a firm with a widely dispersed shareholding, it is the professional management that determines the objectives. And it cannot be assumed that the interests of the management and the owners will always be identical. The salaries paid out to management is only one of the areas where the interests of the owners and the managers may not coincide. In contrast to conventional microeconomics, the Gandhian method acknowledges that situations where the control of the firm is the monopoly of any single interest group is a special case and not a universal rule.

Another departure the Gandhian method makes from conventional microeconomics is in the role of models. Conventional microeconomics treats its models as approximations to reality. The value of a model is believed to lie in its ability to explain conditions as they exist. The Gandhian method recognises the importance of such models. But it does not believe that this is the only role for models in understanding microeconomic issues. As we have already noted, it views the firm as a conglomeration of interest groups. As the relationship between these groups keeps changing the method cannot be satisfied with merely understanding conditions as they exist at any given point of time. It must also decide the specific direction in which this relationship should move. Thus even as it certainly needs to understand the conditions that exist, it does not need to endorse them. It would only endorse a system which throws up fair bargains that protect the interests of all who have a stake. The fact that such a system may not exist, is no reason to abandon the effort to move in that direction. Models are then also needed to define the abstract ideal towards which the system should be encouraged to move. The value of the model of the ideal must then be evaluated not only in terms of whether it is immediately possible, but also in terms of whether it is desirable. The fact that Gandhi's efforts to get the owner to act as a trustee for all who had a stake in the company did not work, cannot be an argument against the need for an effective trustee. It is this focus on the interests of all stakeholders that also distances the Gandhian method from other radical theorists who seek to take the control of the firm from one stakeholder, the capitalist, and hand it over to a government that claims to represent another stakeholder, labour.

The difference between an approach that is satisfied with what is and one that also specifies what should be can also be seen in the approaches to the individual outside the firm. Conventional microeconomics is more concerned with understanding the individual as he is. When a conventional microeconomic model assumes a particular behavioural pattern the attempt is to capture one facet of human behaviour, without necessarily endorsing that behaviour pattern. The behaviour of groups of individuals is then determined by seeing how they would react to each other if each of them follows predetermined norms. This approach is not without its difficulties. The number of possible interactions multiply with the addition of each individual to the group. This limits the progress that can be made in predicting the subjective reactions of a group from individual actions. The progress made can be extended by using sophisticated mathematics, particularly game theory. But covering all the possibilities that could arise when individuals of even a small society interact with each other is often beyond the capabilities of even game theory.

The Gandhian method emphasises understanding not just how an individual is likely to behave but also how he should behave. As the focus of the method is on generating ideal behaviour, it would not be too concerned about precise predictions of how individuals would react to each other. Instead, the effort would be to encourage individual behaviour in a direction that would provide ideal consequences for the economy as a whole. In other words, the individual is not a mere reactor to policies, but becomes an instrument in the formulation and implementation of policies. For instance, influencing demand through individual and collective action would be an accepted instrument of policy.

THE GANDHIAN CORPORATION

As much of our analysis so far has been in the context of mainstream economics it would be useful to precede a comparison of the Gandhian method and management theory with a brief outline of how the Gandhian method would apply to a corporation. In keeping with the Gandhian method's focus on the individual, the Gandhian corporation too would begin with the individual. It would recognise that as individuals come together in a corporation they do not lose their individual identity, either within the corporation or outside it. The corporation would then be a conglomeration of individuals, all with their own interests. Some of these interests would be determined within the corporation and some outside it. The interests of the controlling shareholder will be determined not only by the returns he gets from the corporation, but also the returns he could get if he puts his resources to alternative uses. Again, the interests of the worker would be determined not only by his earnings in the corporation, but also his alternative opportunities.

The perception of a corporation as a conglomeration of individuals also implies that there is no reason to confine the analysis to any one set of individuals, whether it is the owner or the worker. Indeed, there is no justifiable reason to confine the interests considered to even just those of the owners and the workers. The interests of all individuals who are affected by the corporation would need to be taken into account. This would involve taking into account the interests of a large number of groups which are not conventionally treated as a part of a corporation, such as the customers of the corporation's products and those displaced by the corporation's projects. In other words, a corporation is a conglomeration of all individuals who have a stake in it. Such a stakeholder corporation would protect the interests of all these individuals.

Treating a corporation as a conglomeration of individual stakeholders has implications for the entire functioning of the corporation. The objectives of the corporation cannot be defined in terms of any single interest. The corporation would ideally pursue goals that benefit all who have a stake in it. There would then be a preference for Pareto optimal goals, that is objectives where at least one of the individuals in the corporation benefits without others losing. But when such an optimal situation does not exist, the choice would be the result of bargaining between different stakeholders. As long as the control exercised on a corporation is unequal, the results of bargaining will also not result in actions that are fair to all stakeholders. An effective stakeholder corporation would therefore require two conditions. First, the stakeholders have to be empowered, both financially and in terms of information, to be able to understand and project their interests. And second, there would be a clear perception of what is fair.

A Gandhian corporation would be committed to these conditions. It would first try to ensure that all stakeholders are in a position to understand and protect their interests. And it would establish a mechanism to ensure that all stakeholders are treated fairly. At the core of this mechanism would the concept of Trusteeship. Those running the company would, ideally, need to run it as a trustee of all the stakeholders. They would need to be aware of all the interests involved and the conflicts between them, and then resolve these conflicts in a manner that is fair, and is seen to be fair. This task would be easier for managers who can look beyond their own personal interests. The ideal managers would then be those who can distance themselves completely from the fruits of their actions. Such an ideal manager would, of course, never exist in the real world. But the distance from such an ideal would be a valuable input in deciding the quality of a management.

A commitment to representing the interests of all stakeholders would influence the management's approach to specific problems. Any action the management of a corporation takes would immediately affect one or more of the stakeholders. Cutting costs through lower wage rates would affect labour, doing so through lower input costs would affect the suppliers of inputs, and so on. If the management represents all stakeholders it must choose the action that represents the fairest trade-off between the interests of different stakeholders. This fairness must be reflected not only in the consequences of that action, but also in the means of that action. A management must choose an action not only on the basis of the goodness of its consequences, but also in terms of the goodness of the action itself. In other words, an action must be consistent with a given morality. And it must be transparent enough to be seen to be consistent with that morality.

The focus on all stakeholders also alters the perception of the immediate surroundings of a corporation. When the interests of a corporation are perceived in terms of the interests of its owners alone, the immediate surroundings tend to be limited to a certain area; to the area in which its owners operate. But when we take all stakeholders into account, they could be more dispersed both geographically and in terms of their activities. Several of these stakeholders may even be operating a variety of activities. A corporation with a global presence would have stakeholders spread out across national boundaries and across a variety of activities. The immediate surroundings of the corporation would then be the immediate surroundings of each of these stakeholders. The requirement of the Gandhian method that the objectives of a corporation should be determined by its immediate surroundings would then mean deciding the desirable consequences for each of the corporation's stakeholders spread out across the world.

The emphasis on the interests of all stakeholders also internalises issues that are sometimes treated as external to the corporation. To the extent that those affected by a change in the environment have a stake in a corporation whose actions affect the environment, they would be one of the stakeholders. Their interests would then be internal to the corporation's decision-making process. Similarly, the emphasis on fairness would internalise ethical considerations. The Gandhian corporation would seek to develop and follow a clear set of ethical norms rather than wait for it to be imposed on the corporation by external forces, such as the legal system. It would see its emphasis on ethical principles as an asset rather than a liability. It would advertise its ethical practices in a way that builds its corporate brand equity. Its advertising would focus on specific actions that both reflect its ethical functioning as well as touch a chord with its audience. It could even intervene in larger social processes to take society in a direction that both benefits its stakeholders as well as is good in itself.

In treating the firm as an interactive part of a larger social and economic situation, the Gandhian method has more in common with management theory than it has with microeconomics. The Gandhian method shares with management theory a commitment to the primacy of action. In both these approaches actions cannot always be indefinitely postponed merely because of inadequate knowledge. And the role of knowledge too is similar. For managers, as with the Gandhian method, the primary benefit of knowledge comes from it being an aid to action.

The focus on action also contributes to a more interactive method. As with practitioners of the Gandhian method, managers too need to be extremely sensitive to the external environment. They cannot afford to build plans for their corporation in isolation from the trends around them. They need to be aware of the possibility of 'externalities', like a protest by an environmental group completely disrupting their plans. Consequently, they are also sensitive to the possibility of influencing external opinion. Thus advertising finds a very much more critical role in management theory and practice than it does in conventional microeconomics. The need for interaction between the firm and the outside world is reflected in the perception of the firm itself. There is little or no attempt to treat the firm as a homogenous entity. As with the Gandhian method, the firm is treated as an organisation of individuals. Indeed, the behaviour of individuals within an organisation forms a critical part of management theory.

Despite this significant common ground between the Gandhian method and conventional management theory, there remain several differences. In the Gandhian method the primacy of action is built on philosophical foundations. In the case of management theory, on the other hand, it is essentially an occupational hazard. Managers have to come up with actions that can best address a specific situation that they are to manage. This difference is reflected in the perception of the role of managers. The Gandhian method focuses on what the role of the manager should be, while management theorists are content with accepting the role as it is. For years management theorists went along with Henri Fayol's view that the function of managers was to plan, organise, command, coordinate and control (see Fayol, 1949). But the moment Henry Mintzberg found that these functions were rather low in the priorities of managers, it was considered sufficient reason to abandon Fayol's perception of the function of managers (see Mintzberg, 1973). There was little or no attempt to check whether managers should focus on the functions identified by Fayol, even if they did not currently do so. For management theorists *what is* clearly has precedence over *what should be*.

The difference between *what is* and *what should be* has its impact on the attitude to the control of a corporation. Management theory is, what may be called, control-neutral. Management theorists are generally quite content to deal with those who control a corporation. Issues such as takeovers, stakeholder interests and corporate governance do receive considerable attention. But much of management theory operates as if they are not affected by these issues; as if it does not matter who controls the corporation. The behavioural school, the management science school, the contingency approach and the situational approach are all designed to be implemented irrespective of who controls a corporation. In the process they tend to use a minimalist approach towards the stakeholders who do not have control over the corporation. The interests of the stakeholders are only to be met as a means of avoiding pressure on the corporation. The inclusiveness of the Gandhian method, on the other hand, would focus on the link between the nature of control and specific management practices. It would emphasise that a privately owned firm would be inclined to protect the interests of the owner/controller outside the firm; but a corporation with a large public holding may find it more difficult to adopt such a position. The Gandhian method would also not be consistent with a minimalist approach to meeting the needs of stakeholders. It would seek to create an effective and fair system of deciding on actions that best meet the interests of all its stakeholders. Such comprehensiveness is an asset in the competition for the attention of stakeholders, particularly when an individual has more than one stake in the corporation. A stockholding employee also has a stake in the profit of the corporation. An environmentally conscious consumer too has dual stakes in the company. Meeting the interests of one set of stakeholders could then have a spill-over effect in the competition for another set of stakeholders. When there is an employee stock option plan in place, an increase in profits helps attract shareholders as well as employees. Similarly, environmental consciousness reaches out to not just those affected by the impact of the corporation's activities on the environment, but also to environment conscious consumers.

The emphasis on what should be, rather than confining analysis to what is, is sometimes interpreted as a limiting factor of the Gandhian method. By emphasising the need for Trusteeship as well as the empowerment of all stakeholders, the Gandhian method may seem to be relying on conditions that rarely exist on the ground. This would strengthen the impression of the Gandhian method being an idealistic one. It is important therefore to emphasise once again the distinction in the Gandhian method between reality and the ideal. The ideal, which can never be reached, exists only as a pointer to the direction in which a management should seek to move. It is, of course, possible for such an ideal to be so far removed from reality that it has little more than theoretical interest. If stakeholders are never going to be in a position to assert themselves, there would be very little reason for anyone to accept the need for Trusteeship, even as an ideal. Indeed, Gandhi's relative lack of success in promoting the idea of Trusteeship in his lifetime could be attributed to the fact that his concept was too far removed from the reality of his times. But the acceptability of an ideal does not remain constant over time. It is quite conceivable that modern corporations are relatively more inclined to protect the interests of all stakeholders than the business houses in Gandhi's time. There are, in fact, two factors that push modern corporations towards recognising the interests of all stakeholders. First, just as all the stakeholders have an interest in the corporation, the company's survival can also depend on each stakeholder. Labour can kill a corporation through strikes, customers can hurt the corporation's sales, suppliers can destroy production schedules, environmentalists can prevent the setting up of new projects, and so on. The company thus has, at some level, to meet the interests of the stakeholders. Second, corporations often have to compete for the same stakeholders. The most obvious case is that of wooing customers. But there are situations where other stakeholders have to be wooed as assiduously. Corporations have found innovative ways of wooing labour, environmentalists, stockists, suppliers, et al. Thus the survival of a corporation in a competitive environment forces it to move towards meeting the interests of all its stakeholders.

Another major point of departure for the Gandhian method from conventional management theory is in the role of models. Management theorists share with conventional economists a tendency to treat models about specific relationships as approximations to the entire reality. These models can be very relevant in themselves. Kenichi Ohmae's reasons for the declining influence of national boundaries are certainly convincing. The changing preferences of consumers, the dispersion of technology, the pressure to spread fixed costs over a much larger market base, the need to reduce currency risks and the dangers of protectionism all undoubtedly contribute to globalisation. But he then goes on to imply that these factors are the ones that will dominate the economy by arguing that the completely interlinked global economy is inevitable. As he sees it,

'We are not one big happy family in the world yet,' but the global interlinked economy 'may be closer than we think' (Ohmae, 1990, p. 213). This makes his analysis extremely vulnerable to any change in the opposite direction, or even to these processes leading to new borders. For instance, new divisions could emerge in the markets of the developing countries between those who can afford the products of global companies and those who cannot. As the global companies cater to their consumers they may be crossing national boundaries but would be creating new boundaries within each country.

The Gandhian method would avoid this difficulty as it would determine its desired consequences in terms of the immediate surroundings of the corporation. These immediate surroundings could be spread out in different parts of the world depending on the location of the corporation's different stakeholders. The corporation would then look at all factors that can influence its immediate surroundings. In such an analysis there is clearly room for Ohmae's model, but it would not be the only model to be taken into account. In addition to the trends towards globalisation the analysis would also consider the trends towards greater emphasis on local interests, the pressures of regional blocs and a lot else. It would then be in a position to judge the relative importance of each factor in a specific situation without being committed to a single set of factors dominating all situations. This makes the method very much more sensitive to change due to the emergence of new factors, the re-emergence of old factors or simply due to new forms of interaction between well known factors.

The Gandhian corporation is thus an ideal that can act as an effective guide to real situations. It would obviously be futile to expect such an ideal to exist in the real world. But as the importance of stakeholders in a corporation grows, in fits and starts, the Gandhian corporation would be an effective guide to the direction in which the global corporation is moving.

COMBATING EXPEDIENCY

Underlying the differences between conventional economics and the Gandhian method in both macroeconomics and microeconomics is their contrasting approaches to expediency. Conventional economics has a rather ambivalent attitude to expediency. On the one hand, much of microeconomics functions on the principle that a rational individual would do what is expedient. On the other hand, there is considerable recognition in macroeconomic literature of the problems that result from corruption. This ambivalence would have had its uses if it had led to macroeconomic literature providing a comprehensive analysis of expediency. But this has not been the case. Even in macroeconomics though there are some elements of expediency that are not even recognised as such. It would, for instance, be considered perfectly normal for a policy maker to only consider prescriptions that are based on economic models available at a point of time. The development of economic models in turn could be influenced by the information available at any given point of time. And those collecting information would, in their turn, concentrate on issues that currently fashionable economic models are raising. This cycle of expediency thus limits the questions that are being raised. While there could be the odd economist who comes up with an unconventional economic model, he is typically unlikely to be taken seriously until an unexpected crisis forces mainstream economists to seek new answers. This critical role played by the cycle of expediency in mainstream economics rarely receives much attention.

Economists only take expediency seriously when it degenerates into outright corruption. And even then there are serious limitations in the treatment of corruption. In keeping with the tendency towards segmentation in mainstream economics, the issue of corruption is generally treated in isolation. Economists are often quite aware that corruption is a major factor in an economy for which policy prescriptions are being designed. But the conventional reaction is to develop the policy prescriptions independent of corruption and then exhort the government to minimise, if not eradicate, corruption. The possibility of a continuous interaction between corruption and economic policy is rarely taken into account.

Once it is treated as an isolated specialisation, corruption does not attract the attention it deserves. Often the definitions of corruption are themselves extremely narrow. A popular definition is that corruption is the abuse of public power for private benefit. This definition clearly ignores corruption in the private sector as well as the fact that corruption may benefit, not an individual, but a caste or a community. Other definitions are broader, such as the one that stresses the illegal aspects of all rent-seeking. But such definitions imply that corruption can be controlled merely by making what is illegal, legal. Such an approach removes much of the social stigma attached to corruption, and may even act as an incentive for individuals to carry out illegal activity in the hope that it will be regularised later.

Much of the Gandhian method, on the other hand, focuses on reducing the scope for expediency. Expediency is treated in its entirety rather than merely when it is a part of an illegal activity. The focus on expediency as a whole ensures that the method could reject actions that cannot be considered illegal or even immoral. It would not, for instance, allow policy makers to concentrate on factors about which information happens to be more easily available. The choice of factors to be considered would have to be determined entirely in terms of their impact on the consequences. The method also focuses on ethical rather than legal principles. In areas where the two sets of principles do not coincide it is the ethical that will prevail. This approach goes against strategies based on wooing those who have adopted unethical practices, such as amnesty schemes for tax evaders. The emphasis on the ethical will also rule out any strategy that aims to reduce corruption by making the illegal, legal. In other words, the Gandhian method not only recognises the role that expediency can play, but also stresses that this being an ethical problem can only be fought through morality.

* * *

The Gandhian method thus departs from the conventional in economics at a number of points. These points of departure occur over such a wide range of areas that it would be a special case each time a choice that is considered pragmatic is consistent with the Gandhian method. The extent of these differences is also an indication of the vast distance between a pragmatic putting together of specialised views and a genuine inclusive view of the economy.

NOTES

1. One of the critical components of the agricultural strategy that led to the Green Revolution in India was the guaranteed procurement of wheat and rice by agencies of the central government. The procurement prices were relevant not just for the grains that were actually procured but for the rest of the sales of these crops as well. As the farmers could always sell to the procuring agencies, the prices offered by these agencies became the de facto floor price for rice and wheat.
2. The World Development Report of the World Bank, as indeed most other international reports, focuses primarily on national data, though the experts making the report are obviously quite aware of the variations within each national economy.
3. While the IMF and the World Bank may have the independence to decide on whether to support a country engulfed by an economic crisis, their ability to do so is determined by the funds provided by a few national governments.
4. For instance, as a part of a popular defence of large dams, B.G. Verghese argues that 60 per cent of the water used in Delhi comes from the Bhakra system. Verghese (1999, pp. 53–54).
5. The role of ideology is sometimes blurred by the fuzziness that surrounds the concept. It is 'widely agreed that the notion of "ideology" has given rise to more analytical and conceptual difficulties than almost any other term in the social sciences' (Abercrombie et al., 1980, p. 187). The term has been used in a variety of ways and often has a multitude of dimensions (Apter, 1992). In conventional economics though the term ideology generally refers to a set of consistent beliefs that can act as thumb-rules to understand the economy.
6. This is evident, for instance, in the concept of reform outlined by Michael Lipton. 'There are two main concepts of reform: market and redistributive. Unless markets perform exceptionally well, with few restrictions, distortions or information problems, market reforms are desirable—often essential—for efficient (and frequently for poverty reducing) development. Unless everybody has access to key resources, especially of land and of the "children's rights" needed to ensure genuine access to human capital, redistributive reform is highly desirable—often essential—for poverty reduction, and often for any but the most sluggish growth in real income per person' (Lipton, 1994, p. 31).

6

In Practice

We began our outline of the Gandhian method by pointing out that it was built on the cornerstone of the primacy of action. It was the primacy of action that prompted us to evaluate each situation from the point of view of the policy maker rather than the eclectic theorist. It was action that defined our path to comprehensiveness, with the focus being on all elements of an action instead of knowledge alone. And the focus on consequences too implied an evaluation of the actions that generated the consequences. This outline of the Gandhian method would then be incomplete without considering, at least in brief, a specific action in a real life economy. Exploring a specific action will allow us to identify the main points at which the Gandhian method would have followed a different course. The specific economic action chosen here is the Indian Budget presented in July 1991 by the then Finance Minister, Dr Manmohan Singh.

There are several reasons for this choice. The Budget that year was presented in the midst of one of the most significant economic crises in post-Independence India. The official Economic Survey for 1990–91 acknowledged persistent fiscal imbalances, weak balance of payments and a double digit inflation. These pressures were accentuated by the Gulf crisis through a higher oil import bill, a decline in exports and the threat of a decline in remittances from West Asia. The situation thus called for a carefully worked out policy response that would reflect the official method of understanding the economy. The Budget of July 1991 did that and more. It came as close as you can get to a single document outlining the entire philosophy of India's economic reforms. For a variety of reasons, including a delay in the election process caused by the assassination of the former Prime Minister, Mr Rajiv Gandhi, the economic crisis was allowed to reach near-flashpoint, by the time Dr Manmohan Singh presented his Budget. And though the response to this crisis was laid out in several policy statements, including a new industrial policy announced on the same day as the Budget, it was the Budget speech that provided an outline of the strategy underlying the reform.

The Budget's attractiveness as an action worth exploring was enhanced by the fact that it was the work of an academic and administrator-turned-politician. Dr Manmohan Singh's reputation till the 1991 Budget was primarily that of an academic and administrator. And this reputation did not completely abandon him even though he spent the years following the Budget as a politician. His deep roots in academia and administration ensured that the Budget represented a very wide range of sources of economic ideas in India. Taken together with the ideas of its critics in academia, the debate on the Budget covered almost the entire ground in conventional economics in India.

The dominance of Dr Manmohan Singh over the entire process of crafting, and implementing, that Budget also helps our focus on a specific economic action. In a situation where economic policies are formulated by one set of individuals and implemented by another set, there could be some difficulty in working out a consistent pattern that fully reflects the ideas of the formulators and the intentions of those implementing the policy. There is always the risk of leaning too heavily on the ideas of those formulating the policy or, alternatively, on the perceptions of those implementing it. But in the case of the Budget of July 1991, Dr Manmohan Singh ruled over both the process of formulation of the ideas underlying the Budget as well as its implementation. His Budget speech can then be treated as the consistent exposition of that particular action.

THE INDIAN BUDGET OF JULY 1991

In evaluating Dr Manmohan Singh's Budget speech in July 1991 we enter an area that has already been the subject of intense scrutiny. Indian Budgets, as a rule, receive a great deal of attention within the country. They are the vehicle Indian finance ministers have come to use to outline their macroeconomic perspectives. And the attention received by the July 1991 exercise has, quite understandably, been even greater. It has been acknowledged to be not merely the response to the mid-1991 crisis but also the first step in the process of economic liberalisation in India. This widespread attention should normally have made our task easier as it has led to a conventional wisdom emerging about the main contours of the Budget. But much, if not all, of this analysis focuses on evaluating the success of the exercise, with or without the benefit of hindsight. While such an evaluation is obviously important it does not quite meet our requirements. Our interest in the action captured in the Budget speech is to explore the method it uses to understand the economy and then intervene in it. We must then begin with a summary of the methodology implicit in the Budget. And this methodology is best captured by looking at all the elements of the action that was the Budget 1991. We need to begin by considering the object of the knowledge used in the Budget. We would then be in a position to outline the method of arriving at the knowledge used in the Budget. This method would be influenced by the individuals who are arriving at this knowledge. We could then move to looking at the prescriptions in the Budget. This would include the means the Budget speech outlined to intervene in the economy. We could then focus on the budgetary exercise itself before we finally consider the influence of those implementing the Budget.

When knowledge is gathered for a budgetary exercise it is rarely with any single object. The knowledge can be related to improving the efficiency of specific instruments of taxation; it could target reducing inequalities in the economy or a variety of other individual goals. But specific Budgets sometimes have an overriding object. And this was, arguably, true of the July 1991 Budget. Coming as it did in the midst of a major economic crisis, it was that crisis that defined the focus of the Budget. The entire exercise, including the knowledge used in the Budget, appeared to have the objective of dealing with the crisis. When other objectives were mentioned, say, in relation to agriculture, there were very few concrete measures in the Budget to suggest that these were among its primary goals. Dr Singh, in fact, began his Budget speech with a sharp focus on the economic crisis.

> The new government, which assumed office barely a month ago, inherited an economy in deep crisis. The balance of payments situation is precarious. International confidence in our economy was strong until November 1989 when our Party was in office. However, due to the combined impact of political instability witnessed thereafter, there was a great weakening of international confidence. There has been a sharp decline in capital inflows through commercial borrowing and non-resident deposits. As a result, despite large borrowings from the International Monetary Fund in July 1990 and January 1991, there was a sharp reduction in our foreign exchange reserves. We have been at the edge of a precipice since December 1990 and more so since April 1991. The foreign exchange crisis constitutes a serious threat to the sustainability of growth processes and orderly implementation of our development programmes. Due to the combination of unfavourable internal and external factors, the inflationary pressures on the price level have increased very substantially since mid-1990 (Singh, 1991, p. 1).

Dr Singh's method of gathering knowledge to deal with this crisis consisted primarily of reducing the analysis to a set of key factors. To begin with, the crisis itself was reduced to being primarily one of pressure on the balance of payments and the threat of soaring inflation. These pressures were in turn linked to a large fiscal deficit. This deficit pushed up the rate of inflation and since Indian goods were then more expensive, it had an adverse impact on the balance of payments. Reducing the fiscal deficit called for a variety of measures. Subsidies had to be reduced, the burden the public sector placed on the Budget had to be slashed and the tax system had to be reformed. At the same time the balance of payments deficit demanded that Indian industry be made more competitive in the world economy. And, though it was not explicitly emphasised, the balance of payments would also benefit if a liberalised Indian economy attracted foreign investment. In Dr Singh's words:

> The origins of the problem are directly traceable to large and persistent macro-economic imbalances and the low productivity of investment, in particular the poor rates of return on past investments. There has been an unsustainable increase in Government expenditure. Budgetary subsidies, with questionable social and economic impact, have been allowed to grow to an alarming extent. The tax system still has many loopholes. It lacks transparency so that it is not easy to assess the social and economic impact of various concessions built into its structure. The public sector has not been managed in a manner so as to generate large investible surpluses. The excessive and often indiscriminate protection provided to industry has weakened the incentive to develop a vibrant export sector. It has also accentuated disparities in income and wealth. It has worked to the disadvantage of the rural economy. The increasing difference between the income and expenditure of the Government has led to a widening gap between the income and expenditure of the economy as a whole. This is reflected in growing current account deficits in the balance of payments (Singh, 1991, p. 2).

In presenting this theory as the knowledge on which the Budget was based, Dr Singh chose not to use the determined conviction of an ideological crusader. Instead, he presented his chosen knowledge in terms that were much less prone to controversy. As the knower of the situation that demanded the reforms of his Budget, Dr Singh took on an aura closer to that of an academic above the debate on the Indian economy rather than an active participant in the debate.

> As we enter the last decade of the twentieth century, India stands at the cross-roads. The decisions we take and do not take, at this juncture, will determine the shape of things to come for quite some time. It should come as no surprise, therefore, that an intense debate rages throughout the country as to the path we should adopt. In a democratic society it could not be otherwise. What can we learn from this debate? (Singh, 1991, p. 9).

Dr Singh went on to answer this question in a way that further reduced the scope for controversy. He systematically underplayed the extent to which his analysis was a departure from the old orthodoxy about the Indian economy. Even as he presented a stark picture of the magnitude of the economic crisis, he took care not to suggest that he was demanding a radical departure from the past. Instead, he presented the crisis as a reflection of the defects in the old perspective that needed to be corrected, without abandoning the perspective as a whole. This was evident in Dr Singh's description of the challenge facing the Indian economy in 1991.

> The challenge we are facing is without precedent. In its initial stages, the Industrial Revolution in the western world concentrated on the creation of wealth, unmindful of the social misery and inequity which characterised this process. The democratisation of the polity came much later. The socialist experiment in charting a new path for accelerated industrial transformation of an underdeveloped economy and polity did achieve considerable success in developing technological and military capabilities, accumulation of capital for rapid industrial growth and human resources development, in countries such as the USSR. But recent developments have shown that this approach too suffered from major

weaknesses, particularly in its allocative efficiency, in the management of technical change, control of environmental degradation and in harnessing the vast latent energy and talents of individuals. In India, we launched an experiment under the leadership of Pandit Jawaharlal Nehru, an experiment which sought to unite the strengths and merits of different approaches to accelerated development of our backward economy. We have achieved considerable success in the field of development, modernisation and greater social equity. However, we are yet far from realising our full potential in all these areas (Singh, 1991, p. 10).

The emphasis on merely correcting inadequacies within the old framework, rather than developing an alternative framework, also prefaced several other cases for reform built in the Budget. Thus the case for reform in the public sector was prefaced with the contention that the 'public sector has made an important contribution to the diversification of our industrial economy. But there have been a number of shortcomings' (ibid., p. 6). Again, 'the widening and deepening of our financial system have helped the spread of institutional finance over a vast area and have contributed significantly to the augmentation of our savings rate, particularly financial savings. This has been a most commendable achievement, but our financial system has developed certain rigidities and some weaknesses which we must address now' (ibid., p. 7).

To further reduce the distance between his analysis and the old orthodoxy, Dr Singh made effective use of the rhetorical tool of appealing to authority. He repeatedly cited the authority of the icons of the earlier era. There were references to Jawaharlal Nehru and Mahatma Gandhi. He even cited concepts used by Gandhi to suggest his view was not very different. He insisted that while he was removing stumbling blocks from the path of those who created wealth, those 'who create it and own it, have to hold it as a trust and use it in the interest of the society, and particularly those who are underprivileged and without means. Years ago, Gandhiji expounded the philosophy of trusteeship. This philosophy should be our guiding star' (Singh, 1991, p. 11). That the Budget had no concrete steps to encourage trusteeship of any kind is a different matter.

To this rather conservative role that Dr Singh defined for himself as an individual gathering knowledge for the Budget, he added a centralised means of implementing his prescriptions. Some of this centralisation was inherited. The Indian Budget had become the prime instrument of economic policy well before 1991. The finance ministry had already gained a virtual monopoly in economic policy making with other institutions like the Planning Commission becoming increasingly irrelevant. But Dr Singh consolidated this centralisation of economic policy making within the finance ministry and the Budget it formulated. He did little to rejuvenate institutions like the Planning Commission and allowed an impression to gain ground that policies in other ministries, like industries and commerce, were being formulated by the finance ministry.

This centralisation was also reflected in the role, or more precisely the absence of a role, for the states and local bodies in the liberalisation process. There was little in the Budget to indicate a major devolution of power. There was no attempt to define a new autonomous role for the states in the liberalisation process. At best, states were urged to follow the path set by the centre right down to the minutest detail. For instance, the Budget proposed setting up the office of a chief commissioner for non-resident Indians. The finance minister then urged the state governments to also establish an office of a commissioner for non-resident Indians. The question of defining a precise role in the process for local bodies was never addressed. Nor did Dr Singh even consider the possibility of using nongovernmental organisations to implement the processes identified in the Budget.

This centralisation of economic power in the hands of an economist-administrator-turned-politician would normally have required a major change in political equations. While Dr Singh did enjoy a measure of support from those who hoped to benefit from reforms, there were some very critical constituencies that a thorough-going process of reforms could alienate.

Changes in both agriculture and the public sector would have called for much greater political support than Dr Singh had in 1991. Dr Singh side-stepped this problem by merely ensuring that the means he used to intervene in the economy kept the impact on these politically sensitive constituencies to a minimum. These sectors could not be left completely untouched by the Budget. The need to reduce the fiscal deficit led Dr Singh to limit both the fertiliser subsidy as well as the allocations for public sector units. But he was careful not to make these measures the first step in a process of wide-ranging reform. The limited allocations to the public sector were not followed up with a clearly worked out plan for reforming that sector. And in agriculture too limiting the fertiliser subsidy was not to be a part of a larger reform moving away from a policy of intervention in agriculture that depended heavily on procurement prices. On the contrary, farmers were to 'be compensated for the proposed increase in the price of fertilisers through suitable increases in procurement prices' (Singh, 1991, p. 14).

The expediency of Dr Singh's means was not confined to the political sphere. In other spheres too he saw no harm in taking the expedient option. He introduced an amnesty scheme to mop up black money. Under this scheme, illegal funds could be deposited with the National Housing Bank, where 40 per cent of the deposits would be deducted and the rest could be withdrawn by the depositor. The 'monies deposited would be provided complete immunity from enquiry and investigation' (ibid., p. 26). Indeed, he was comfortable enough with the principle of expediency to speak about it only half in jest.

> Few would disagree that I am one of the most harassed Finance Ministers in recent times. To perform the onerous task before me, I need support from the Press. As a gesture of goodwill, I propose to exempt standard newsprint from import duty which is, at present, Rs. 450 per metric ton. I have already proposed to bring down the rates of import duty on certain specified machinery and equipment required by the printing and newspaper industry to the levels that were

obtaining before 15th December, 1990. The monetary limit of duty free import of photographic goods by accredited cameramen of the Press is being raised from the present level of Rs. 30, 000 to Rs. 60, 000. These proposals involve a revenue loss of over Rs 9 crores in a full year (Singh, 1991, p. 41).

The choice of a means based on centralised expediency ran the risk of hurting the credibility of the entire exercise. In order to develop credibility as the individual who would supervise the implementation of the Budget—the doer as it were—Dr Singh used a combination of measures. To begin with, he sought to ease the pressures of being a political novice by identifying himself as a close follower of the Nehru–Indira Gandhi–Rajiv Gandhi lineage that dominated the then ruling Congress Party. There were repeated references in his Budget speech to Jawaharlal Nehru, Indira Gandhi and Rajiv Gandhi. And his support for this lineage was not restricted to rhetoric alone. He also decided to contribute Rs 100 crore, to be given in five annual instalments of Rs 20 crore, to the Rajiv Gandhi Foundation, despite the extreme pressure on the fiscal deficit.

Dr Singh then went on to present the economic situation as a national crisis. The impression of a crisis calling for immediate action was strengthened by the use of words like 'there is no time to lose' (ibid., p. 3) or 'without decisive action now, the situation will move beyond the possibility of corrective action' (ibid., p. 2). Care was also taken to portray the crisis as one affecting equity as much as growth. Hence: 'Inflation hurts everybody, more so the poorer sections of our population whose incomes are not indexed' (ibid., p. 3); or: 'If we do not introduce the needed correctives, the existing situation can only retard growth, induce recession and fuel inflation, which would hurt the economy further and impose a far greater burden on the poor' (ibid., p. 4).

The emphasis was not just on the crisis, but also on the fact that it was a national one. He thus made effective use of nationalist rhetoric. He presented his choice of globalisation as a nationalist one. By going out of his written speech to quote Urdu nationalist poetry, he sought to place his Budget on par with other acts of nationalism. He also appealed to the authority of the 'founding fathers of our Republic' (Singh, 1991, p. 6) as well as, more specifically, Pandit Jawaharlal Nehru and Gandhi. And he went on to embellish his entire exercise with a touch of optimism, as in the manner in which he concluded the Budget speech.

> Sir, I do not minimise the difficulties that lie ahead on the long and arduous journey on which we have embarked. But as Victor Hugo once said, 'no power on earth can stop an idea whose time has come' I suggest to this august House that the emergence of India as a major economic power in the world happens to be one such idea. Let the whole world hear it loud and clear. India is now wide awake. We shall prevail. We shall overcome (ibid., pp. 47–48).

The choices Dr Singh made in each of the elements of his action delineated the lines within which the specifics of the Budget had to function. The objective of the entire exercise, the knowledge base he gathered, the approach he adopted as the knower, the means he chose to implement the Budget and the role he adopted as the person in charge of implementing the Budget, all affected the specifics of the Budget itself. The choice of the macroeconomic crisis as the primary object of the exercise ensured the Budget would focus on the balance of payments and fiscal deficits. The main task then was to find measures that would reduce the deficits in not just the short term, but also over the medium and longer term. On the fiscal side this called for measures to control expenditure and to raise revenue. And on the balance of payments side, measures had to be identified that would increase the inflow of foreign exchange.

The choice of specific measures was determined by the core model Dr Singh chose. This model was built around the principle that the prominent role played by the state in the Indian economy since the 1950s had outlived its utility and that future progress lay in reducing the role of the state. Thus government expenditure was to be reduced by slashing subsidies and cutting down support for the public sector. Increased revenue was to be generated not by increasing rates of taxation but by encouraging greater compliance through lower rates. The balance of payments crisis was also to be addressed not by increasing duties but by reducing them. Lower customs duties were expected to make it easier for exporters to import critical inputs. Increased imports were also, over time, expected to force domestic industry to become more competitive. And as the Indian economy opened up foreign capital was expected to find it a more viable destination; thereby further easing the pressure on the balance of payments. The macroeconomic crisis in mid-1991 made Dr Singh wary of giving the economy a strong dose of these measures. The income tax rates, for instance, were left untouched. But the finance minister did use the Budget speech to explicitly commit himself to reducing these rates—a commitment he stood by in the following years.

A METHODOLOGICAL CRITIQUE

Evaluations of the July 1991 Budget speech years after it was delivered are bound to be influenced by the benefit of hindsight. It is difficult to avoid judging the quality of Dr Singh's judgements, at least partially, by the actual course of events that followed the Budget. But evaluating the quality of Dr Singh's judgements is of little use to us in our comparison of his method with the Gandhian one. The errors of judgement he may have made could as easily have been made by economists using the Gandhian method as well. Focusing on these errors of judgement may make an effective critique of Dr Singh's exercise, but it would tend to hide the adverse effect on the Budget of his method. Our purpose would be better served if we focus on the methodological aspects of Dr Singh's Budget. Our critique would then be confined to those weaknesses of Dr Singh's strategy that can be traced to specific methodological choices he made. And while we may not be able to completely remove the benefit of hindsight, we will try to minimise this influence by focusing on those consequences that could be directly traced to his Budget speech in July 1991.

A major weakness of the action captured in the July 1991 Budget was that it focused almost exclusively on aspects of the economic crisis that were directly reflected in macroeconornic parameters. We cannot underestimate the extent of the macroeconomic imbalance in July 1991. But these were not the only areas of concern in the economy. The poverty-ridden rural economy cried out for greater attention. While the share of agriculture and allied activities in national income was declining quite sharply, the proportion of the population dependent on agriculture was not declining as rapidly. The Budget, however, focused primarily on the balance of payments and fiscal deficits. It had little time for agriculture. The few occasions when agriculture did enter the picture, the strategy was defined in terms of the requirements of the balance of payments and fiscal crises rather than in terms of the pressures on agriculture. There was thus an attempt to cut fertiliser and other agricultural subsidies, without addressing the pressures that generated a demand for these subsidies.

The preoccupation with macroeconomic imbalances was also reflected in the approach to the rest of the world. Even when dealing with exports and imports the focus was primarily inward-looking. Thus though the Budget did make a major move towards cutting tariff barriers, there was no effort to link these changes with India's position in the Uruguay round negotiations. The prospect of negotiating a change in India's tariff rates with other countries in the Uruguay round of GATT negotiations was considered an unacceptable loss of sovereignty. Even without the benefit of hindsight, it should have been possible to predict the costs of such an approach. Working out the reform process in isolation meant that India would not benefit from these changes in international negotiations. With the country's international negotiators continuing with the old brief of least change, there was always the possibility of India fighting for causes in international trade negotiations that it had already abandoned at home. And despite the magnitude of the change introduced at home, India would continue to present the image of a country unwilling to give up outdated practices. Such an image was bound to adversely affect India's ability to attract allies even among the developing countries.

The faith in core theories too had predictable costs. There was always the risk that the faith in a theory, strengthened by a situation in which it was valid, would lead to the theory being followed even when it was no longer appropriate. Dr Singh had a Monetarist's faith in a tight money policy. This faith was useful in the initial years of reform when the removal of restrictions could lead to a spurt in spending and inflation. But continuing with a tight money policy even after production could rise to meet higher demand brought in the risk of stifling demand and hence growth. Moreover, there was the risk of the core theory ignoring promising approaches. The theories Dr Singh chose tended to treat areas like the conservation of power as worthy only of pious statements rather than concrete action.

The approach Dr Singh adopted towards presenting the knowledge base on which he built his Budget was also not beyond debate. By presenting himself as being above the debate he created the impression that all the knowledge he used was scientifically proved. Thus even his judgements were to be treated as scientific facts. The resultant faith in the knowledge he had chosen made him quite insensitive to factors that happened to fall out of the purview of his core theories. We have already noted that these factors were not a few remote exceptions. They covered a variety of critical areas, particularly agriculture and allied activities. But with the judgements being seen as scientific facts, the Budget did not leave open the option of changing tack.

Disguising judgements as scientific facts, combined with ignoring the moral dimension, substantially increased the scope for corruption. A central judgement in Dr Singh's exercise was that the state had failed and had to be replaced by private initiative. Once this judgement was presented as a scientific fact, it was believed that all the problems associated with state ownership would disappear with liberalisation. The proposed reduction in the areas where the state was dominant was expected to correspondingly reduce the scope for corruption. But those who saw this as a judgement rather than a scientific fact would have recognised that this need not always have been the case. While liberalisation could reduce the scope for corruption in some areas, it increased the scope for corruption in others. A spurt in stock market activities before an adequate regulatory mechanism was put in place was an invitation for wrong-doing. The sequencing of liberalisation too was a potential source of corruption. There was the possibility of illegal payments being made both to delay an industry's liberalisation as well as to hasten it.

The approach to implementation reflected in the Budget was also not free of potential problem areas. The decision not to ruffle political feathers was undoubtedly influenced by the fact that Dr Singh was a novice in politics and believed that he had enough on his plate in economic issues alone. But this approach also meant that aspects of the economy that called for political change would be largely ignored. For instance, one of the contributors to a growing fiscal deficit was the rising revenue deficit. This increase was due, in no small measure, to the growing size of the government coupled with populist measures. Tackling this problem, however, was always going to be difficult without a clearly worked out political agenda. As Dr Singh did not have such an agenda, there was always the very real risk that his efforts to control the fiscal deficit would stop short of comprehensive reform of the way the government functioned.

Thus even without the benefit of hindsight it was possible to pick out aspects of the Indian Budget of July 1991 that could distort the process of reform it introduced. These problem areas could be traced directly to the methodology Dr Singh used to formulate and implement his Budget. We can now see how an alternative, Gandhian, method would have handled these challenges.

A GANDHIAN ALTERNATIVE

The first step in building a Gandhian alternative is to decide what should be the objective of the entire exercise. What should be the desired consequences of the reform and how should these consequences be prioritised? As our contention has been that the Gandhian method can work with a variety of subjective positions, we would be best served by accepting the desired consequences, and their prioritisation, implicit in the Budget presented by Dr Manmohan Singh in July 1991. The inclusiveness of the Gandhian method would, of course, make it difficult to restrict the exercise to dealing with the crisis of macroeconomic imbalances as Dr Singh did. The chosen desired consequences would need to deal with all aspects of the economy, including the morality implicit in such a choice. Dr Singh's Budget speech does not explicitly give us such a set of desired consequences. But it may be fair to treat his references to the 'massive social and economic reforms needed to remove the scourge of poverty, ignorance and disease' (Singh, 1991, p. 47) as a statement of the desired consequences. Such a view would also be consistent with his listing of the failures of the pre-reform economy which includes protection, accentuating disparities in income and wealth and working to the disadvantage of the rural economy (ibid., p. 2).

Converting these broad statements of intent into more specific desired consequences would call for a further departure from Dr Singh's method. The fact that Dr Singh chose the national Budget as the major instrument of his economic intervention fits in with the conventional wisdom among economists that reform is essentially an exercise carried out at the national level. Local policies are, at best, derived from the national. In the Gandhian method, on the other hand, the focus is on the individual in the context of the local economy. All measures are chosen on the basis of the impact on the individual within the local economy. The removal of poverty, ignorance and disease would undoubtedly require measures not only at the local level, but also at the levels of the larger region, the nation, the regional bloc and the global. But all these measures would have to be continuously evaluated in terms of the impact on the individuals within the local economy.

It is worth reminding ourselves that this focus on the local economy does not make it the only unit of analysis. As we have already noted, the factors influencing the local economy may lie at the national or international level. And understanding processes at those aggregate levels may call for models where the unit of analysis is national or even global. What is more, the principle of Swadeshi implies that the very concept of what is local can keep changing depending on the issues being considered. While considering the final price paid by an individual, the term local would refer to the economy in his immediate vicinity, such as a village or a firm. When considering the impact global trade negotiations have on this price the term local could mean the national economy.

The objective of a Gandhian Budget in July 1991, would then have been to contribute to the removal of poverty, ignorance and disease for all individuals in their local context.

In order to realise this overriding objective, all the issues that affected poverty, ignorance and disease would need to be addressed. Since the realisation of this objective would have been jeopardised by the crisis of macroeconomic imbalances, the crisis certainly needed to be addressed. But it was equally clear that the overriding objective could not be met merely by restoring the macroeconomic balance. There was thus a need to not just address the crisis, but to go beyond it.

In building a knowledge base to look at the crisis and beyond, the Gandhian alternative would have resisted any temptation to reduce a complex reality into a core economic model. In identifying the factors that could influence poverty, ignorance and disease, it would have made an effort to be inclusive. The inclusiveness would have taken the Gandhian alternative to several areas which Dr Singh chose to ignore. To begin with, the exercise would have been very much more comprehensive in terms of the sectors it analysed. In particular, it would have given the rural economy very much more attention than Dr Singh did. Within the rural economy it would have analysed the trends in agriculture in some detail. And even within agriculture it would have paid greater attention to areas that were not the main beneficiaries of the Green Revolution, like dry land farming. A Gandhian alternative would have acknowledged that these areas remained backward precisely because the Green Revolution package of credit and technology, which worked so well in irrigated areas, was not sufficient to boost growth in dry land regions. The magnitude of investment required was greater than what an individual farmer could borrow. And since dry land technology works best when implemented over a large region, the small scale of farming operations also became a constraint. Individual small farmers had little incentive to invest in technologies that had to be implemented over large tracts of land owned by other farmers. A Gandhian alternative would have developed mechanisms that would help dry land farmers pool their limited resources to invest in large-scale technology and then share the benefits of this technology.

The comprehensiveness would have also extended to the factors that could generate a particular desired consequence. The response to the power crisis, for instance, would have concentrated not only on increasing generating capacity, but also improving the efficiency of utilisation of power. The value of a unit of power saved would have been more than the value of a unit of power generated because of the transmission and distribution losses between the point of generation and the point of consumption. This difference would have been used to provide incentives for power conservation, including duty cutbacks on pumpsets or lighting systems that make more efficient use of power. Given the high transmission and distribution losses in India in 1991, these incentives would have been quite substantial. In addition, the distortions in the system that encouraged the use of machinery that made inefficient use of power would have been removed. This would have required not just increasing the awareness of inefficient machinery, but also reducing subsidies on power prices that lower the incentive to save power.

The comprehensiveness would have led to a greater awareness of costs that are sometimes ignored. While the Gandhian alternative would have recognised the value of higher investment, it would have been sensitive to its costs as well. The benefits to the individual of a higher earning would be seen in the context of costs like the damage to the environment of his immediate surroundings or the social and cultural costs of physical displacement of the individual. The alternative would thus have developed a system of incentives at the national level to encourage industries that are sensitive to the environment. The Gandhian alternative would have also ruled out projects where the environmental and other costs to the local population are greater than the benefits to the same individuals. If a particular project was viable because of its benefits outside the local area, as would have been the case in most power projects, a large enough share of the benefits would have been transferred back to the local area, so as to meet the Swadeshi requirement of improvement in the condition of the immediate surroundings.

The Gandhian method would also not have underestimated the social costs of transforming a predominantly agricultural economy into a predominantly industrial one. History has shown that these costs can be cataclysmic as in the case of the industrial revolution in Britain or Stalin's collectivisation. And the potential for similar costs in India should be evident from the fact that the transition of the Indian economy from agriculture to industry by drawing labour into big cities would involve the shifting of several hundred million individuals. A Gandhian alternative would thus have had as one of its objectives a minimisation of the costs of the transition from an agrarian economy to an industrial one. A major portion of these costs emerges from physically removing individuals from their social and cultural moorings and transplanting them in an unknown urban situation. Minimising these costs would then require minimising the physical displacement of individuals in the transition to an industrial economy. The zero displacement option would be for each village to develop its own industrial base. But the minimum viable scale of economic operations would make this option unviable. The next best option would be to focus on small towns. If a large enough number of small towns are developed across the country, and the links between the small town and the village are improved, it would be possible for a substantial section of the rural population to work in industries in these towns even as they continue to reside in the familiar environment of their village. The Gandhian alternative would thus have focused on creating a vast network of modern, industrialised small towns. It would have built on the inherent benefits of these small towns, such as the ability to tap low cost rural labour or even capital generated by the Green Revolution. It would have strengthened these inherent advantages by developing much stronger linkages between the village, the small town, the urban metropolis and the global economy. This would have involved improving transportation networks, whether by roadways, railways, riverways or air. Modern communication networks would have been developed to allow even remote villages to become a part of the global village. And these linkages would have been given an economic content by improving the ability of individuals in remote villages to tap the global economy. With the revolutionary changes that have taken place in global communication technology it would have been technologically feasible to, say, tap potential computer programmers in remote villages with the help of satellite links.

In putting together such a broad set of interlinked policies, the Gandhian method would have been clear that there were judgements involved in the choice of the specific policies. Each of the policies could not then be treated as the only scientifically valid option. Instead, the Gandhian alternative would have been open to the possibility of a particular theory not quite working along expected lines. It may then require other measures to ensure it works better. And if these measures fail, the Gandhian alternative would be quick to withdraw that specific policy initiative. For instance, the Gandhian alternative could have gone along with the view that one way of improving the efficiency of resource utilisation is to keep prices down through increased competition. The reduced profit margins would have been expected to make the manufacturer more sensitive to costs. The Gandhian method would then have actively promoted measures that increase competition. In most cases, and certainly in the situation prevailing in India in 1991, this would have meant opening up the economy to foreign competition. But the Gandhian method's distrust of grand principles would have ruled out taking it for granted that the opening up of the economy would necessarily increase competition. It would have also been sensitive to the possibility of large companies coming in and wiping out local competition, thereby increasing the degree of monopoly. A Gandhian alternative policy for the Indian economy in 1991 would thus have ensured that along with the opening up of the economy there was a simultaneous reform of the anti-monopoly laws, making them more suited to deal with monopolistic actions in a market economy. And, if despite all these efforts, there was an increase in the degree of monopoly, the Gandhian alternative would not be averse to reconsidering the basic premise that opening up the economy leads to greater competition.

The inclusiveness of the Gandhian method would have also influenced the means it used to intervene in the economy. It would have made it reluctant to rely excessively on any single instrument of intervention. The Gandhian method would have recognised that the earlier excessive reliance on the state had resulted in the creation of severe bottlenecks. But it would not have believed that these bottlenecks could be removed by merely intervening at the national level. For the market to work effectively restrictions on the free flow of goods and services at all levels would have had to be removed. And these restrictions were not merely administrative ones. The free flow of goods was also restricted by the absence of basic infrastructure, like roads connecting remote villages or the lack of an adequate number of vehicles to ply on those roads. A free market option in the Gandhian alternative would have included removing these restrictions.

This inclusive view of a free market would have also ensured that reform was not seen as merely a matter of reducing government control. It also required a series of other initiatives to make the market more efficient. The Gandhian alternative would have been very sensitive to the need for regulatory mechanisms to ensure that the withdrawal of the government did not lead to increased corruption. Ideally, it would have liked self-regulatory mechanisms through which each individual or group of individuals takes it upon themselves to stay within the law of the land, and to be seen to be doing so. But it would also have been clear that this was an ideal. As such it may never have been realised. It was thus essential that the government also took on a major role in creating regulatory mechanisms. And this would not have been the only new role the government would have to take on. The Gandhian alternative would have also recognised many other points in the economy where it needed to intervene.

Take the need to reach the benefits of growth to the more remote corners of the economy. Assimilating these local economies into the mainstream economy would have required encouraging producers of goods and services to look at these markets. There could, for instance, have been a set of simultaneous initiatives in both the urban and rural markets. The urban initiative could have aimed at increasing the demand for non-material products, including those that cater to an individual's spiritual needs. As a greater share of the urban mind and resources went into these products, the manufacturers of material products could have been pushed into looking at the rural market. The government could have also used its energies towards helping industry identify products in rural markets. There has been, for instance, a tendency in rural India to use the tractor for transportation. This could be interpreted as a latent demand for other more efficient systems of mass transportation. Similarly, the huge wastage in vegetables produced in a large number of widely dispersed villages could be seen as an indicator of the demand for small food preservation units. And if urban industry remained sceptical about the potential of the rural market, the Gandhian alternative would have focused on rural capital. It could then have gone so far as to demonstrate this potential to urban industry by tapping rural capital that was generated as a result of the Green Revolution.

The Gandhian method would, in fact, have given a great deal of importance to exploring new options. It would have tried to put together a wider range of sources of capital. The task of raising capital would not have been confined to merely wooing large foreign capital to step in to make up for shortfalls in state capital. A Gandhian alternative would have recognised the potential of cooperatives to pool in widely dispersed local capital, particularly in the rural areas. It would also have explored the potential to shift savings from relatively unproductive assets like gold holdings to avenues where the capital could be more easily tapped for industrial use. The potential of such a shift in savings was quite substantial in 1991, as India was becoming a major consumer of gold. In fact, it had by the second half of the 1990s become the world's largest consumer of gold. And even within foreign capital there would have been an effort to tap the resources of the common people in the advanced countries. The potential for small foreign capital being put to productive use in a developing country like India was enhanced by the fact that the value of the rupee in dollar terms was, and is, very much more than its value was in terms of purchasing power parity. The purchasing power of savings in advanced countries was thus very much larger when converted into rupees. Even middle class investors in the advanced countries would have had sufficient resources to invest in, say, part-ownership of a drip irrigation network. A Gandhian method would have developed such possibilities, emphasising not just the profitability of such ventures but also the moral satisfaction to a small investor in an advanced country of helping lift families above the poverty line in some of the poorest parts of the world. It could have also used the global network of NGOs in making the required linkages between relatively poor farmers in backward regions and small investors in the advanced countries.

Even as it found new roles for the government, the Gandhian alternative would not have lost sight of the fact that the state was only one player in the economy. Most economic decisions had to be implemented by individuals outside the employment of the state. This meant that it was not just the government but all organisations that had to be sensitive to signals from a variety of sources, from the local economy to the global one. One way of increasing this sensitivity would be to encourage organisations that listened to all those who had a stake in it. This is more likely to happen in organisations that are controlled by stakeholders. Ideally, these organisations would retain their sensitivity to local conditions even when they grow into global giants. The Gandhian alternative would thus have encouraged the development of stakeholder organisations. The managements of these organisations would be able to distance themselves from any set of stakeholders and represent all stakeholders. These managements would provide a modern version of Gandhi's concept of Trusteeship. The task of developing such modern stakeholder organisations in a relatively backward industrial climate that existed in India in 1991 was not an easy one. But a Gandhian alternative would have taken a significant step in this direction by encouraging the distancing of ownership from control.

It is clear from the choice of the objective of the Gandhian alternative, from the knowledge gathered for it, from the approach of those who gather that knowledge and from the means adopted to intervene in the economy, that there are judgements involved at virtually each step. The Gandhian method would have been very sensitive to the possible costs of imposing an individual's judgements on the economy. It would thus have sought to arrive at a bargained consensus wherever possible. The Indian economy in July 1991 may not have had a faultless mechanism to arrive at a bargained consensus on economic issues. But as a vibrant democracy it had several political mechanisms, including the party system and Parliament, that could have been used as mechanisms to arrive at a bargained consensus. Thus far from limiting the role of the political class in economic policy making, as Dr Singh did, the Gandhian alternative would have actively involved the political class in resolving all potential conflicts of interest.

In working out the specifics of the Budget proposals that would be consistent with these other elements of the action, the Gandhian method would have been acutely aware of the precise role the Budget played in economic policy. It would have recognised that the Budget dealt with just the finances of the central government. An overall strategy to deal with the problems of poverty, ignorance and disease would require initiatives from a variety of other agencies as well. There was a role for governments at other levels from the state down to the village. And agencies outside the government too had a role to play. The Budget was but one component of a policy that required other initiatives both within the government and outside. It may not even have been the most important component of that policy initiative. All that was then required of the Budget was that it was consistent with the larger initiative and provided the central government with the resources needed for the exercise.

Once the Budget was, as it were, put in its place, the very perception of the crisis would have been altered. There would no longer be the risk of getting preoccupied with the elements of the crisis that are directly reflected in the Budget, like the fiscal deficit, at the cost of other elements requiring equally urgent attention, like rural poverty. The Budget would have recognised that the crisis areas that had to be addressed had to include not just the balance of payments and the fiscal deficit, but also health, education and poverty. This broader perception of the crisis would have influenced the approach to each specific aspect. The approach to reducing the fiscal deficit, for instance, would have had to be consistent with the approach to sectors like health, education and those having a direct impact on the quality of life of the poor. Controlling the fiscal deficit by merely slashing expenditure on critical activities like rural health or rural drinking water would not have been acceptable to a Gandhian Budget.

The need to take an inclusive view of the expenditure reduction exercise would have been reflected in the attitude to subsidies. The Gandhian economic policy maker would have gone along with Dr Singh's assessment that allowing subsidies to grow unchecked was not a sustainable option. But he would have been much more sensitive to the possibility of an across the board cut in subsidies hurting the prime objectives of removing ignorance, disease and poverty. Rather than merely slashing subsidies, the focus of a Gandhian alternative would have been on reducing the demand for subsidies. This could have required measures outside the Budget. Take the food subsidy in India during the 1990s. The subsidy is the result of the government distributing foodgrains through the public distribution system at a price that is lower than what it costs to procure the grain. The government's commitment to support farmers through continuously growing procurement prices ensured that there was a continuous pressure on this gap to widen. The quick, and politically easy, way to cut this subsidy was to simply raise the price of the grain sold in the public distribution system. But this approach was bound to drive the poor out of the public distribution system. Indeed, if we take into account the fact that the carrying costs of Indian government agencies tended to be higher than that of private enterprises, even some of those who could afford the grain may have preferred the open market. The government was then left with the paradox of huge foodgrain stocks even as the nutrition levels of sections of the population remain less than optimal.

One way out of this paradox would have been to separate the strategy for the public distribution system from the support strategy for farmers. The government would then have needed to procure only the quantity of grain needed for a public distribution system targeted at the poor alone. It could have further cut costs by stocking more of relatively lower priced inferior cereals that the really poor would not mind consuming. At the same time, the strategy to support farmers could have focused on a variety of other measures that reduced the costs to farmers, including local low cost initiatives to improve rural infrastructure. Most of these changes in the public distribution system as well as the support strategy for farmers would have fallen outside the purview of the Budget. But the success of the measures outside the Budget would have reduced the burden of the food subsidy on the Gandhian Budget.

The inclusiveness of the Gandhian method would also have been reflected in the changes within individual sectors. This would be evident in the approach of the Gandhian alternative to the public sector. In terms of the need to bring about an immediate reduction in the fiscal deficit it may have been enough to merely remove budgetary support to individual public sector units. Even if the units did not survive the cut in their funding, they would no longer be a burden on the Budget. But the Gandhian method would have recognised that this was a short-term approach that could be counterproductive in the medium term. The increased unemployment would have led to social pressure which would have, in a democracy, translated into a demand for subsidies. The more meaningful approach would then have been to link the reduction in budgetary support to a transformation of the public sector unit into an effective stakeholder corporation. The corporation could then have been made more efficient and flexible enough to move into the more profitable sectors of the economy. It is only when all these efforts failed that the corporation would be liquidated. And the employees, as well as others dependent on the corporation for their livelihood, would be provided the benefit of a safety net.

An inclusive view of expenditure control would have also recognised the links between the economic need to reduce expenditure and the political environment in which it had to be done. Rather than seeing the task of controlling expenditure purely as an economic exercise, the Gandhian alternative would have recognised the political dimensions of this task. It was obviously extremely difficult to cut expenditure in a system of political patronage that relied heavily on government funds. It was therefore necessary to first bring about the political changes that would have made such patronage less critical to the success of a politician. And once the demand from the political class for patronage related expenditure diminished, the task of controlling revenue expenditure would have become that much easier.

In terms of generating revenue too the Gandhian Budget would have gone further than Dr Manmohan Singh did. The Gandhian method's continuous search for options would have made it explore all possibilities of raising revenue. It would have agreed with Dr Singh that a lower rate of income tax could generate higher revenues due to better compliance. But it would have recognised the limits of a strategy that merely seeks to woo potential tax-payers. There was always the danger that some of the incentives used to woo potential tax-payers could prove counterproductive in the long run. The amnesty scheme for those with unaccounted money may have been an effective means of gaining revenue in the short run. But it confirmed the belief that such schemes would be introduced periodically. And as long as there is a realistic prospect of such schemes being introduced in the future, individuals could well decide to skip taxes secure in the knowledge that there will be an opportunity to legalise their funds at a later date. The strategy to improve compliance in a Gandhian Budget would thus not have included measures that could not be made consistent with a given moral position. Nor would it have been confined to merely reducing the rates of taxation. It would have recognised the need for a more comprehensive strategy to improve compliance, including exerting social pressure on those not paying taxes.

On the balance of payments front too, a Gandhian Budget would have taken a wider view. While it would have agreed with Dr Singh that efforts must be made to attract foreign investment as well as to make Indian industry more competitive, it would have explored more options than was attempted in the Budget of July 1991. Its measures to attract foreign capital would have included specific concessions for NGOs that linked small contributions in the developed world to specific projects for the poor in India. And its approach to competition would not have been confined to measures in the Indian economy. It would have tried to change conditions in the global markets in a way that would help Indian products compete more effectively. In order to achieve this objective it would have been willing to link the lowering of tariff barriers in India to specific concessions from the advanced world, either bilaterally or during the course of global negotiations.

Once the pressure on the fiscal deficit and the balance of payments deficit had eased, it would have been possible for the Gandhian Budget to support a major thrust in the areas it had focused upon: education, health and poverty alleviation.

7

In Conclusion

We can now return to the question with which we began this exercise. What is it about the methodology economic policy makers use that prevents them from anticipating a crisis? The simple answer is: The practice of reducing reality to a single model. Models are an essential part of an economist's armoury. They help isolate relationships and subject them to rigorous scrutiny. But when a model is projected as an approximation to reality, it has an inbuilt weakness. The rigour of a model is built on its abstracting a few relationships from reality and assuming away the rest. Even the most complex models necessarily leave out several factors. And when a crisis is caused by factors that are left out of the model, policy makers using that model cannot anticipate it.

This rather obvious problem has not quite received the attention it deserves, largely because of economists' fascination with ideology. When a model based on one set of factors fails, economists come up with another model based on another set of factors. As the latter model is based on what has already happened, it will better explain the given situation. Economists then present the latter model as the new scientific truth. But as and when the situation changes so that the factors underlying the old model regain importance, the latter model has to once again give way to the old one. Mainstream economics has thus tended to swing between monetarism, Keynesianism and a number of other models variously described as belonging to the Right or the Left. When economists have been dissatisfied with the continuous swinging of the ideological pendulum they have tended to adopt a more pragmatic approach. This approach gives them the freedom to choose between conflicting models. But Pragmatism does not offer any safeguard against expediency. Equally important, there is the possibility of a crisis being caused by factors that all the models used by economists at a particular point of time have chosen to ignore. We can then have a crisis which is not anticipated by any major economist, as happened in Asia in 1997.

There is then clearly a need for a method that does not attempt to reduce reality to a single model. At the same time the method must not compromise on the rigour offered by models. The Gandhian method seeks to meet these apparently contradictory objectives by shifting the focus of analysis to the consequences. Instead of searching for a model that can explain a particular situation, the emphasis is on identifying a set of desired consequences. The policy maker can then take into account all the factors that influence these consequences. And since the focus is on the action to achieve a particular desired consequence, the analysis covers all the elements of an action from the theoretical formulation to the implementation. In evaluating various options the policy maker will need to consider the relationship between specific factors. These relationships would be better understood with the help of rigorous models. The policy maker would then have to put together these different models to develop the whole picture. For this picture to be complete the analysis cannot be restricted to areas where rigorous models are available. Where such rigorous models are not available, other less rigorous sources would have to be tapped. This inclusive picture would then provide the basis for the policy maker to choose the appropriate action. As this approach uses all the knowledge provided by rigorous models at a point of time, it does not compromise on rigour. But it also does not limit itself to what can be proved with an acceptable degree of rigour at a given point of time.

This shift in focus from the core model underlying a situation to the consequences raises new questions that need to be addressed. The obvious question is about the apparent justification of any action, as long the consequences are good. The Gandhian method addresses this question through its inclusiveness. As it does not see any action in isolation, an action is not evaluated in terms of its predetermined consequence alone. All possible consequences are taken into account. Since the very fact of an action being taken instantly changes a given situation, it is a consequence in itself. As was pointed out in an earlier chapter, lowering costs may be a means to an end, but it can also be seen as an end in itself. There is then no difference between means and ends. And the goodness of the consequences automatically implies the goodness of the actions as well.

The focus on the goodness of the consequences also raises questions about what is to be considered good. This will obviously be decided by the morality that exists at a particular point of time. But this morality is not absolute. It can, and does, change both over time and across people. The Gandhian method recognises the difficulty in defining an absolute morality. It therefore recognises that it can function only with a relative morality. In defining this relative morality there will be a tendency for each individual to emphasise the rights that suit him or her. A morality for the society as a whole would then be arrived at through a process of bargained consensus. In arriving at this bargained consensus it is often tempting to define the relative morality at unrealistically high levels. But when relative morality is out of tune with society there will be a greater tendency to accept immoral actions. A policy maker who is expected to follow moral standards that are out of tune with what society accepts, could find it difficult to implement his policies. He would then be tempted to discard morality altogether on the grounds of being pragmatic. It is therefore imperative that the relative morality on the basis of which the goodness of consequences is to be judged is closely related to what a society can accept at a point of time. That is to say, a relative morality must not promise rights the society cannot guarantee. For instance, the right to work is an extremely desirable right, but few societies are able to guarantee it. The Gandhian method's answer to this challenge is to link each right to a duty. The right to work would be linked to the duty to work efficiently so that the economy could grow at a pace that generates an increasing number of jobs. The moment a duty is not performed the corresponding right cannot be protected. The relative morality must then only be defined in terms of the rights that a society is willing to do its duty to protect.

The danger in this approach is, of course, that lower and lower standards of relative morality can be set on the grounds that society cannot accept higher standards. For this downward spiral to be avoided the relative morality followed by a policy maker must be defined by those whose moral credentials cannot be challenged. And in order to ensure that those defining relative morality are not being sanctimonious, the Gandhian method makes the distinction between the moral, immoral and the non-moral. While an immoral person would break the norms of morality, those who simply follow these norms would be non-moral. In order to be considered moral, the person had to back his morality with sacrifice. A person who did so would not be inclined to unnecessarily lower moral standards. He or she would then have the moral right to define a relative morality that is in tune with what a society can achieve. And once this relative morality is defined, it would create the basis for deciding on the goodness of consequences.

Our case for consequentialism has been built primarily on its inclusiveness. It encourages taking into account all factors that can influence consequences. But clearly no analysis can take into account all consequences in the universe. The Gandhian method thus focuses on a chosen set of desired consequences. It excludes consequences other than the ones chosen. The analysis then becomes very sensitive to the choice of consequences. And the policy maker will tend to be preoccupied with consequences that directly affect him or those whom he represents. There is thus an inherent tendency to prefer the immediate surroundings. The Gandhian method explicitly recognises this inherent tendency, developing it into the concept of Swadeshi. Through this concept the method advocates a focus on immediate surroundings when choosing the desired consequences. But the immediate surroundings would depend on the level of aggregation. The immediate surroundings for a rural individual would be his village, while for a nation it could be a regional bloc. The precise components of an aggregation too would vary from issue to issue. An individual's immediate surroundings for a religious issue would be his religious group, while for an economic issue it could be all groups, irrespective of their religion, in the local economy. There is thus always a variety of groups at different levels of aggregation, each with its own set of desired consequences.

To arrive at a common set of desired consequences at any level of aggregation, the Gandhian method advocates a bargained consensus. The method recognises the prerequisites of such a consensus. If the consensus is not to be unequal, all groups must be empowered. If the system of bargaining is not to break down, there must be a tolerance of opposing views. The ability to arrive at a consensus would improve if there are more options. For the consensus to be accepted it would have to be seen to be fair. And the Gandhian method believes that if those involved in the consensus were not seen to be attached to the fruits of that consensus, there is a greater chance of their judgements being considered fair.

The explicit role that the Gandhian method provides for judgements, brings to the fore the question of dealing with subjectivity. The Gandhian method makes no attempt to reduce subjectivity. It is quite clear that an appropriate action to achieve a desired consequence cannot be based only on what is objectively known at a point of time. The focus of the method is thus on improving the quality of subjective judgements. The first step in this direction is to clearly demarcate the role of subjectivity. While the understanding of any situation will involve the use of both reason and faith, the method emphasises that faith cannot get precedence over reason. Faith will then only play a role where the answers are not provided by reason alone. Within this limited role the quality of subjectivity would be improved if the policy maker is not attached to the consequences of his actions. And the scope for expediency would be reduced through the use of betting quotients to provide a transparent index of the quality of a policy maker's subjective judgements.

The shift from the search for a core model that explains a situation to focusing on the consequences clearly covers a wide range of issues. In addressing these issues the Gandhian method often has to adopt positions that are not conventional. A great deal of the emphasis of the method, for instance, is on identifying the questions that must be raised, while much of conventional economics concentrates on finding answers to questions that are taken as given. As we have seen in earlier chapters the departures from convention are not confined to issues that have been raised in the debate on economic methodology. They extend to other conventions in economics that have not received very much critical scrutiny, like the focus on national economies. Indeed, the departure from convention would extend to the very way economists make out their case. This is quite evident from the present exercise itself. The influence of the Gandhian method is reflected in the way we have built our case.

The inclusiveness of the method has widened our canvas. This exercise has traversed several specialised fields of study. Indeed, the journey from the concept of knowledge to the specifics of India's economic reform in the 1990s is a long one. It has involved putting together the results of a number of specialised analyses available in each field. Such an exercise has necessarily involved an element of judgement. The subjectivity involved in this exercise is evident at several places. Gandhi's ideas themselves have been interpreted in a way that more traditional Gandhians may not accept. The explicit acceptance of subjectivity has determined the rhetoric of this exercise. No effort has been made to suggest that the arguments here represent the sole scientific truth. The entire exercise is, in fact, quite sensitive to the possibility that its arguments are fallible. The nature of inclusive economics that is outlined here cannot then be final. But if this exposition of the Gandhian method leads to a wider recognition of the need for economics to become more inclusive, it would have served its purpose.

Select Bibliography

BOOKS

Abercrombie, Nicholas, Stephen Hill and **Bryan S. Turner** (1980) *The Dominant Ideology Thesis*. London, George Allen & Unwin.

Arestis, Philip and **Victoria Chick** (eds) (1992) *Recent Developments in Post-Keynesian Economics*. Hants, Edward Elgar.

Ayer, A.J. (1982) *Philosophy in the Twentieth Century*. London, Unwin Hyman.

Backhouse, Roger E. (ed.) (1994) *New Directions in Economic Methodology*. London, Routledge.

Blaug, Mark (1980) *The Methodology of Economics. Or How Economists Explain*. Cambridge, Cambridge University Press.

Boland, Lawrence A. (1982) *The Foundations of Economic Method*. London, George Allen and Unwin.

—— (1989) *The Methodology of Economic Model Building: Methodology after Samuelson*. London, Routledge.

Boulding, Kenneth E. (1992) *Towards a New Economics. Critical Essays on Ecology, Distribution and Other Themes*. Aldershot, Edward Elgar.

Cahoone, Lawrence E. (ed.) (1996) *From Modernism to Postmodernism. An Anthology*. Cambridge (Mass.), Blackwell.

Chandravarkar, Anand (1989) *Keynes and India. A Study in Economics and Biography*. London, Macmillan.

Corrsetti, Giancarlo, Paolo Pesenti and **Nouriel Roubini** (1998) *What Caused the Asian Currency and Financial Crisis?* Downloaded from the Internet, March.

Dalton, Dennis (1998) *Gandhi's Power. Nonviolence in Action*. Delhi, Oxford University Press.

Dasgupta, Ajit K. (1993) *A History of Indian Economic Thought*. London, Routledge.

Datta, Bhabatosh (1978) *Indian Economic Thought. Twentieth Century Perspectives 1900–1950.* New Delhi, Tata McGraw-Hill.
Devitt, M. (1991) *Realism and Truth,* 2nd edn. Oxford, Basil Blackwell.
Easwaran, E. (1997) *Gandhi the Man.* Mumbai, Jaico.
Eichner, Alfred S. (ed.) (1983) *Why Economics is not a Science.* London, Macmillan.
Fayol, Henri (1949) *General and Industrial Management,* translated by Constance Storrs. London, Pitman.
Feyerabend, Paul (1978) *Against Method.* London, Verso.
Fischer, Louis (1954) *Gandhi. His Life and Message for the World.* New York, Mentor.
Gadgil, Madhav and **Ramachandra Guha** (1993) *The Fissured Land. An Ecological History of India.* Delhi, Oxford University Press.
Gandhi, Mohandas Karamchand. (1958–93) *Collected Works of Mahatma Gandhi.* Vols 1–100. New Delhi, Publications Division, Government of India.
———. (1996) *The Bhagvadgita.* Delhi, Orient Paperbacks.
Gerrard, Bill and **John Hillard** (eds) (1992) *The Philosophy and Economics of J.M. Keynes.* Aldershot, Edward Elgar.
Henderson, Willie, Tony Dudley-Evans and **Roger Backhouse** (eds) (1993) *Economics and Language.* London, Routledge.
Hicks, John (1979) *Causality in Economics.* Oxford, Basil Blackwell.
Hutchison, T.W. (1938) *The Significance and Basic Postulates of Economic Theory,* reprinted 1965. New York, Augustus M. Kelley.
——— (1981) *The Politics and Philosophy of Economics. Marxians, Keynesians and Austrians.* Oxford, Basil Blackwell.
Johnson W.J. (trans) (1994) *The Bhagavad Gita.* Oxford, Oxford University Press.
Keynes, John Maynard (1973) *A Treatise on Probability. The Collected Writings of John Maynard Keynes. Volume VIII.* London, Macmillan.
——— (1983) *The General Theory of Employment, Interest and Money.* London, Macmillan.
Keynes, Milo (ed.) (1975) *Essays on John Maynard Keynes.* Cambridge, Cambridge University Press.
Kuhn, Thomas S. (1962) *The Structure of Scientific Revolutions.* Chicago, The University of Chicago Press.
Lange, Oscar and **Fred M. Taylor** (1976) *On the Economic Theory of Socialism* (edited by Benjamin E. Lippincott). New Delhi, Tata McGraw-Hill.
Maki, Uskali, Bo Gustafsson and **Christian Knudsen** (eds) (1993) *Rationality, Institutions and Economic Methodology.* London, Routledge.

Mintzberg, Henry (1973) *The Nature of Managerial Work.* Englewood Cliffs, New Jersey, Prentice Hall.
Nagel, Ernest (1984) *The Structure of Science. Problems in the Logic of Scientific Explanation.* Delhi, Macmillan.
Ohmae, Kenichi (1990) *The Borderless World.* New York: Harper Business.
Ormerod, Paul (1994) *The Death of Economics.* London, Faber and Faber.
Pani, Narendar (1994) *Redefining Conservatism. An Essay on the Bias of India's Economic Reform.* New Delhi, Sage.
Passmore, John (1968) *A Hundred Years of Philosophy.* Middlesex, Penguin.
Pieterse, J.N. (ed.) (1992) *Emancipations, Modern and Postmodern.* London, Sage.
Popper, Karl R (1959) *The Logic of Scientific Discovery.* London, Routledge.
––––––– (1961) *The Poverty of Historicism.* London, Routledge and Kegan Paul.
––––––– (1983) *Realism and the Aim of Science. From the Postscript to the Logic of Scientific Discovery,* edited by W.W. Bartley, III. London, Hutchison.
Ramanadham, V.V. (ed.) (1993) *Privatisation. A Global Perspective.* London, Routledge.
Rawls, J. (1971) *A Theory of Justice.* Cambridge, Mass., Harvard University Press
Robbins, Lionel (1984) *The Nature and Significance of Economic Science,* 3rd edn. London, Macmillan.
Schumacher, E.F. (1977) *Small is Beautiful.* New Delhi, Radha Krishna.
Sen, Amartya K. (1979) *Collective Choice and Social Welfare.* Amsterdam, North Holland.
Sen, A.K. (1984) *Resources, Values and Development.* Oxford, Basil Blackwell.
––––––– (1988) *On Ethics and Economics.* Oxford, Basil Blackwell.
Sills, D. and **R. Merton** (1991) *International Encyclopedia of the Social Sciences, Vol. 19 (Social Science Quotations).* New York, Macmillan.
Singh, Manmohan (1991) *Speech of Shri Manmohan Singh (Minister of Finance) Presenting Central Government's Budget for 1991–92,* 24 July. New Delhi, Government of India.
Tarlo, Emma (1996) *Clothing Matters: Gandhi and the Recreation of Indian Dress.* London, Hurst & Company.
Wood, John Cunningham (ed.) (1983) *John Maynard Keynes. Critical Assessments,* 4 volumes. London, Croom Helm.

ARTICLES

Apter, David E. (1992) 'Democracy and Emancipatory Movements: Notes for a Theory of Inversionary Discourse', *Development and Change,* 23(3): 139–73.

Backhouse, Roger, E. (1994) 'The Lakatosian Legacy in Economic Methodology' in Roger E. Backhouse, (ed.), *New Directions in Economic Methodology,* pp. 173–91. London, Routledge.

Blaug, Mark (1994) 'Why I am not a Constructivist. Confessions of an Unrepentant Popperian' in Roger E. Backhouse (ed.), *New Directions in Economic Methodology,* pp. 109–36. London, Routledge.

Braithwaite, R.B. (1973) Editorial Foreword to *A Treatise on Probability. The Collected Writings of John Maynard Keynes. Volume VIII.* London, Macmillan Press.

——— (1975) 'Keynes as a Philosopher' in Milo Keynes (ed.), *Essays on John Maynard Keynes,* pp. 237–46. Cambridge, Cambridge University Press.

Cahoone, Lawrence E. (1996) 'Introduction' in Lawrence E. Cahoone (ed.), *From Modernism to Postmodernism. An Anthology,* pp. 1–23. Cambridge (Mass.), Blackwell.

Caldwell, Bruce, J. (1994) 'Two Proposals for the Recovery of Economic Practice' in Roger E. Backhouse, (ed.), *New Directions in Economic Methodology,* pp. 137–53. London, Routledge.

Carabelli, Anna (1992) 'Organic Interdependence and Keynes's Choice of Units in General Theory' in Bill Gerrard and John Hillard (eds), *The Philosophy and Economics of J.M.Keynes,* pp. 3–31. Aldershot, Edward Elgar.

Dasgupta, Partha (1992) 'Nutrition, Non-Convexities and Redistributive Policies' in John D. Hey (ed.), *The Future of Economics.* Oxford, Blackwell.

Dasgupta, Sugata (1989) 'The Core of Gandhi's Social and Economic Thought' in J. Hick and L.C. Hempel (eds), *Gandhi's Significance for Today,* pp. 189–202. London, Macmillan.

Frankel, Jeffrey A. (1998) The Asian Model, the Miracle, the Crisis and the Fund. Paper delivered at The US International Trade Commission, 16 April.

Friedman, Milton (1972) 'Comments on the Critics', *Journal of Political Economy,* 80: 906–50.

Gerrard, Bill (1992) 'Human Logic in Keynes's Thought: Escape from the Cartesian Vice' in Philip Arestis and Victoria Chick (eds), *Recent Developments in Post-Keynesian Economics,* pp. 1–16. Hants, Edward Elgar.

Gerrard, Bill (1993) 'The Significance of Interpretation in Economics' in Willie Henderson, Tony Dudley-Evans and Roger E. Backhouse (eds), *Economics and Language,* pp. 51–63. London, Routledge.

Gustafsson, Bo (1993) Preface in Uskali Maki, Bo Gustafsson and Christian Knudsen (eds), *Rationality, Institutions and Economic Methodology,* pp. ix–xi. London, Routledge.

Hands, D. Wade (1993) 'Popper and Lakatos in Economic Methodology' in Uskali Maki, Bo Gustafsson and Christian Knudsen (eds), *Rationality, Institutions and Economic Methodology,* pp. 61–75. London, Routledge.

Hoover, Kevin D. (1994) 'Pragmatism, Pragmaticism and Economic Method' in Roger E. Backhouse (ed.), *New Directions in Economic Methodology,* pp. 137–53. London, Routledge.

——— (1995) 'Why does Methodology Matter for Economics?', *Economic Journal,* 105 (May): 715–34.

Krugman, Paul (1994) 'The Fall and Rise of Development Economics' in Lloyd Rodwin and Donald A. Schon (eds), *Rethinking the Development Experience: Essays Provoked by the Work of Albert O. Hirschman.*

——— (1998a) What Happened to Asia? Paper presented to a conference in Japan in January 1998. Downloaded from the Internet.

——— (1998b) Two cheers for formalism. Forthcoming in *Economic Journal.*

Leontief, Wassily (1983) Foreword in Alfred S. Eichner (ed.), *Why Economics is Not a Science.* London, Macmillan.

Lipton, Michael (1994) Two Concepts of Reform: Can Liberalisation help the Poor? Visiting lecture, *Asian Development Bank,* 1994, mimeo.

Maki, Uskali (1993a) 'Economics with Institutions. Agenda for Methodological Enquiry' in Uskali Maki, Bo Gustafsson and Christian Knudsen (eds), *Rationality, Institutions and Economic Methodology,* pp. 3–42. London, Routledge.

——— (1993b) 'Two philosophies of the rhetoric of economics' in Willie Henderson, Tony Dudley-Evans and Roger E. Backhouse (eds), *Economics and Language,* pp. 23–50. London, Routledge.

McCloskey, Donald N. (1994) 'How to do a Rhetorical Analysis, and Why' in Roger E. Backhouse (ed.), *New Directions in Economic Methodology,* pp. 319–42. London, Routledge.

Morishima, Michio (1992) 'General Equilibrium Theory in the Twenty-first Century' in John D. Hey (ed.), *The Future of Economics*. Oxford, Blackwell.

Pieterse, Jan Nederveen (1992) 'Emancipations, Modern and Postmodern' in J.N. Pieterse (ed.), *Emancipations, Modern and Postmodern*, pp. 5–41. London, Sage.

Radelet, Steven and **Jeffrey Sachs** (1998) The Onset of the East Asian Financial Crisis. Paper presented at the National Bureau of Economic Research (NBER) Currency Crisis Conference, 6–7 February.

Rorty, Richard (1996) 'Solidarity or Objectivity?' in Lawrence E. Cahoone (ed.), *From Modernism to Postmodernism. An Anthology*, pp. 573–88. Cambridge (Mass.), Blackwell.

Sachs, Jeffrey (1997) 'Personal View', *Financial Times,* London, 30 July.

Verghese, B.G. (1999) 'A Poetic Licence,' *Outlook,* New Delhi, 5 July, pp. 52–54.

Index

absolutism, disguised, 87–89
abstraction, 63, 96, 97–103
action, 36, 53, 54, 58, 59, 60n6, 94, 115; choice of, 41, 77–87, 190; collective, 28, 123, 126, 146, 150; consequences of, 37, 41, 44, 45, 46, 48, 49, 50, 55, 61, 70, 72, 73, 78, 80, 83, 116, 118, 121, 132, 134, 152, 191; consistency among elements of, 86, 94, 95, 184; effectiveness of, 86; good, 50, 55, 101, 126; immoral, 44, 45, 48, 159, 191; and knowledge, 50–51, 86; local consequences of, 73, 74, 77; moral, 44, 45; and morality, 41, 42, 65, 95; non-moral, 44, 45, 48; pure, 39
action-consequence relationships, 61, 62, 63, 64, 143
ahimsa, 33, 112 *Also see* non-violence
Ambedkar, Dr B.R., 128n15
anarchism, 55
anti-monopoly laws, 181
Asian crisis, 13–14, 17, 24, 25, 33nl, 35n13, 98, 100, 190
attachment, 49
authority, 85, 167
awareness, 68, 69, 70, 78, 126

Backhouse, R.E., 35n20, 127n3

balance of payments, 161, 164–65, 171, 172, 173, 185, 188
bargaining, 67–68, 70, 71; unrestrained, 68
belief, 56, 57; irrational, 106, 107; rational, 105
betting quotient, 57, 58, 59, 87, 113, 117, 121, 194
Bhagvadgita, 36, 37, 50, 51, 52, 53, 60n1, 78, 117, 120
Blair, Tony, 34n8
Blaug, Mark, 99, 108, 128n9
Bolshevik revolution, 85
Boulding, K.E., 32, 132
Braithwaite, R.B., 56, 57

capital, 70, 89, 182; foreign, 183, 188
Carabelli, A., 119
centralisation, 168
chaebols, 34n10
Chauri Chaura movement, 83–84
choice, 28, 39, 41, 54, 64, 83; consequentialist approach to, 38, 43–44
communism, 19, 20, 26, 33, 130, 137
Communist Party, in China, 21
comprehensiveness, 26, 28
conflict, 67, 69; of interests, 74, 124, 131, 136, 146, 184; resolution of, 67, 71, 125–26, 151

Congress Party, 34n8, 60n2
consequences, goodness of, 39, 41, 42, 117, 191, 192; pure, 39; unintended, 123, 132, 136; universal view of, 72
consequentialism, 38, 39, 41, 42, 50, 55, 65, 72, 73, 77, 88, 101, 116, 117, 124, 139, 192; deontological, 91, 127n2
consistency, 86, 94, 95, 101, 114, 115
convention, and method, 129–30
cooperation, 67
cooperatives, 182
corruption, 158, 159, 174, 181
Corsetti, G., 35n19
crony capitalism, 14, 23, 24, 35n17

Dalton, D., 128n10
Dasgupta, Partha, 96
Dasgupta, Sugata, 79–80
Datta, Bhabatosh, 30
decentralisation, 30, 77
devaluation, competitive, 14, 15, 134–35
doles, 124

economy, and the issue of control, 61–62, 82; and state intervention, 19, 20, 81–82, 94–95, 100, 126, 128ns6, 13, 144, 181
empowerment, 68, 69, 70, 71, 74, 146, 155
environment, 48, 60n3, 152–53
equality, 67, 71
ethics, 42, 70, 95, 118, 153, 159
expediency, 27, 35n16, 47, 48, 55, 85, 86, 111, 144, 157–59, 169, 170, 190, 194

fairness, 70, 71, 74, 91, 94, 124, 126, 152, 153
faith, 54, 55, 58, 60, 103, 111, 112, 113, 127, 193
falsifiability, 104, 105, 109, 110, 111, 113, 129

falsification, 28, 59, 108, 111, 113, 127, 129; of hypotheses, 99
fascism, 50
Fayol, Henri, 154
Feyerabend, P., 93–94, 109–10, 112
fiscal deficit, 161, 165, 169, 171, 173, 185, 186, 188
Fischer, Louis, 89n1, 90n2
Fisher, Irving, 17–18, 114
Frankel, J.A., 35n17
free market, 19, 20, 22, 34n6, 40–41, 81, 82, 94–95, 100, 124, 126, 128n6, 144, 181
free trade, 34n7
Freud, S., 107
Friedman, Milton, 119
fundamental rights, 40

Gandhi, Indira, 170
Gandhi, M.K., 29–33, 167, 171; and abstraction, 63–64, 101–3, and decentralisation, 77, 88; and economic rationality, 31; and modern technology, 88; and morality, 42–45, 48; and the primacy of action, *See* Gandhian method; and rationality, 56; and the separation of religion and politics, 60n4; and the state versus market debate, 102; and the use of political symbolism, 31
Gandhi, Rajiv, 162, 170
Gandhian method, 29, 30, 32, 33; abstract ideal in, 64; as applied to a corporation, 150–57; attitude to growth, 138–40; and the choice of appropriate unit of analysis, 75–76; and the choice of problems, 93–96; consistency in, 86; fallibility in, 87; and focus on action, 36, 43–44, 45, 46, 53, 72, 86, 94, 126, 129, 153, 154, 161, 190; focus on consequences, 39, 101, 122, 140–42, 144, 161, 190; and focus on the individual, 67, 77, 147, 150,

183; and focus on local economy, 133, 136; and ideal behaviour, 149–50; and ideals, 89; as idealistic, 49; non-growth objectives of, 139–40; inclusiveness of, 32, 33, 36, 41, 47, 48, 50, 54, 55, 61, 63, 73, 80, 81, 86–87, 95, 112, 122, 126, 127, 145, 155, 176, 177, 181, 186, 191, 194; and subjectivity, 47–50, 112–16
General Agreement on Tariffs and Trade (GATT), 173
General Equilibrium Approach, 16, 18, 21, 22, 24, 25–26, 27, 28, 98
Gerrard, B., 100
globalisation, 30, 156, 170
Gorbachev, M., 19
Green Revolution, 160n1, 177, 180, 182
group formation, 66
Gulf crisis, 161

Heidegger, M., 120
Hicks, J., 114
Hitler, Adolf, 50, 112, 118
human development index, 139, 140
Hume, A., 104
humility, 118
Hutchison, T.W., 98, 128n8
hyper-inflation, 102
hypotheses, testing of, 99

ideology, 18–22, 160n5, 189, 190
imperialism, 34n12
inaction, 50, 60
inclusive method, 27–29, 39
individualism, 66
individuals, cooperation between, 67; focus on, 77 *See* Gandhian method; as an instrument of intervention, 82–83; and resources, 69, 70, 71; role of, 66–67
induction, 104
industrialisation, 88

inequality, 68, 70, 124; gender, 78
inflation, 64, 77, 86, 132, 133, 161, 165, 170, 174; rate, 13, 131
intellectual property rights, 34n11
intentions, good, 44–45, 47, 50
International Monetary Fund (IMF), 160n3, 164
interpretation, 27, 119–21, 127
irony, 84–85

judgement, 65, 71, 81, 87, 114, 184, 193; error of, 47, 88–89, 172; fair, 78; intuitive, 102, 103; quality of, 58, 79, 89, 117; and scientific facts, 174–75; subjective, 47, 50, 53, 55, 59, 60, 89, 115, 193, 194; value, 115, 116

Karma Yoga, 53, 60n6
Keynes, J.M., 56, 57, 100, 104, 114–15
Keynesian economics, 99, 119, 122, 144, 190
khadi, economic activity based on, 69; campaign for, 46, 60n2
King, Martin Luther, 128n10
knowledge, 49, 50–53, 56, 57, 78; fallibility of, 32, 83, 123, 194; incompleteness of, 54; and the knower, 51, 78, 80, 81; limits of human, 104; object of, 78, 94; objective, 112; perfect, 103–4; rhetoric as an element of, 117; subjective, 112; subjective elements of, 51–52, 95; true, 79
Krugman, Paul, 13, 34ns2, 4, 35n18, 93, 96, 97–98
Kuhn, T., 127

Labour Party, in Britain, 21, 34n8
labour power, 70, 89
labour, 70, 89, 149
Lakatos, I., 109, 128n8
Lange, Oskar, 94
Leontief, Wassily, 97

liberalisation, 128n13, 144, 163, 168, 174, 175
Lipton, Michael, 160n6
Lohia, Ram Manohar, 128n15

'mainstream' economics, 22, 23, 27, 29, 32, 38, 59, 140, 158, 189
Maki, U., 97, 117
Marshall, Alfred, 96
Marx, K., 107
Marxian economics, 81, 144
Marxism, 26, 129
'maximin' approach, 43
McCloskey, D.N., 28, 84, 85, 117, 127
methodology, 17, 18, 23
Mintzberg, Henry, 154
misinterpretation, 121
modernisation, 30
morality, 41, 42, 44, 46–47, 48, 55, 65, 85, 87, 88–89, 95 101, 115, 152, 176, 191; absolute, 42, 191; outcome, 42; relative, 42, 47, 65, 191, 192
Morishima, M., 16, 19, 98
most favoured nation status, 19, 34ns7, 11
Mukherjee, Radhakamal, 79–80
multilateralism, 20, 34n11

Nagel, E., 115
Narasimha Rao, P.V., 144
National Housing Bank, 169
nationalism, 171
Nazism, 118
Nehru, Jawaharlal, 167, 170, 171
neo-classical economics, 81
non-attachment, 49, 50, 70, 71, 74, 78, 80, 116, 118, 121
non-cooperation, 67
non-governmental organisations, 168, 183, 188
non-violence, 68, 71, 84, 95, 112, 128n10 *Also see ahimsa*
objective facts, 51, 53, 54

objectivity, 110, 120
Ohmae, Kenichi, 156–57
'optical illusion', 14, 15
options, 46, 47, 64, 65, 69, 71, 77–78, 86, 126, 144, 180, 182, 187, 188, 190, 193
Original Position, Rawls', 91, 127n1
Ormerod, P., 128n5
ownership, and control, 148, 184

participant observation, 80, 116
Peirce, Charles Sanders, 18, 35n16
Pesenti, P., 35n19
Pieterse, J.N., 32, 125
Ping, Deng Xiao, 20, 21, 144
Planning Commission, 168
pluralism, 21, 22, 43, 52–53, 65, 83, 87–88, 95, 123, 145
Popper, Karl, 33, 93, 103, 104, 105, 106, 107, 108, 111, 112, 127, 128n8, 129, 130
post-modernism, 32, 33
pragmatism, as a policy, 24, 35n16, 191; school of, 18, 21, 22, 23, 25, 26, 28, 101, 144, 145, 146, 190
predictability, 25
privatisation, 34n6
probability, 56, 57
prohibition, 88–89
protectionism, 34n12, 72–73, 156
public distribution system, 185–86

rent-seeking, 159
rights, awareness of, 69; and duties, 40, 41, 192; protection of, 39, 40, 41, 66
reason, 54, 58, 103, 111, 112, 113, 193
rationality, 56, 57, 114, 118, 128n11
reality, 59, 63, 64, 89; attitude of Gandhian method to abstractions of, 122, 131, 148, 177; models as approximating, 96–103, 149, 156, 189, 190; perceptions of, 110

rationalism, 110
Rorty, R., 110
Radelet, S., 33n1
Roubini, N., 35n19
Ramsey, F.P, 57
Rawls, J., 91, 127n1
Robbins, Lionel, 128n12
Rajiv Gandhi Foundation, 170
rhetoric, misuse of, 118, 121; role of, 27, 28, 84, 85, 86, 87, 116–18, 127, 170, 194
regionalism, 20, 34n11

Sachs, Jeffrey, 14, 15, 33n1
sacrifice, 45, 47, 48, 85, 192
Salt Satyagraha, 31, 35n22
Sankhya Yoga, 53, 60n6
satisfaction, 69
science, and metaphysics, 106, 107, 111; misuse of, 112; and non-science, 103, 105, 112; and subjectivity, 110
scientific method, 106, 112
secularism, 49
self-interest, 48, 49, 91, 114
Sen, A.K., 35n21, 38, 41–42, 91, 127n2, 128n11
sensitisation, 70
Singh, Dr Manmohan, 20, 144, 161–77 *passim*, 184, 185, 187, 188
situational dimension, 31, 32; sensitivity to, 26–27
solidarity, 110
Special 301 watch list, 34n11
specialisation, 142–43
stakeholder corporations, 151, 187
 Also see stakeholder organisations
stakeholder organisations, 183–84
 Also see stakeholder corporations

stakeholders, focus on, 149, 150, 151, 152, 155
Stalin, J., 109, 110, 112, 179
Stalinism, 50
subjectivity, 47–50, 51, 53, 54, 55, 59, 78, 98, 112, 113–16, 119, 120, 193, 194
subsidies, attitude to, 185–86; cutting of, 171, 173, 185; demand for, 185, 187; fertiliser, 169, 173; food, 185–86
Swadeshi, 63, 72–77, 87, 132, 177, 179, 193

Tarlo, E., 120
Taylor, Fred, 94
testability, 107
Thatcher, Margaret, 34n6
tolerance, 68, 71, 74, 83, 95, 112
Trusteeship, 63, 70–72, 87, 89, 91, 151, 155, 156, 168, 184
truth, absolute, 53, 57, 104, 105, 111, 120; relative, 53, 54, 57, 59, 60, 87, 111, 120, 127

unemployment, 13
unilateralism, 20, 34n11
Uruguay Round, 131, 173

Verghese, B.G., 160n4
verifiability, 104, 105
verification, 104

wants, controlling, 69
welfare economics, 28, 35n14, 43, 72
welfare state, 19
World Bank, 160ns2, 3
World Trade Organisation (WTO), 19, 20, 34ns7, 11, 131

About the Author

Narendar Pani is currently Senior Editor, *The Economic Times,* Bangalore. He has worked with the paper in different capacities since 1987. Prior to joining the *Economic Times,* Dr Pani worked with the *Deccan Herald* (1982–87) and was a Research Fellow at the Indian Institute of Management, Bangalore (1980–82). He was awarded the Citibank Pan Asia Journalism Award in 1992. Besides having contributed a number of articles to specialised journals and written two reports, Dr Pani has previously published *Redefining Conservatism: An Essay on the Bias of India's Economic Reform* and *Reforms to Pre-empt Change: Land Legislation in Karnataka.*

Lightning Source UK Ltd.
Milton Keynes UK
UKHW011851180521
383961UK00001B/112